—— — GOD BLESS — ——

ALSO BY H. L. HIX

POETRY

Chromatic *
Shadows of Houses *
Surely As Birds Fly
Rational Numbers
Perfect Hell

ARTISTS' BOOKS AND LIMITED EDITIONS

This Translucent Tissue (artist's book by Judi Ross)
The Last Hour (artist's book by Egidijus Rudinskas)
Intellectual Pleasures (limited edition by Aralia Press)

TRANSLATIONS

On the Way Home: An Anthology of Contemporary Estonian Poetry,
trans. with Jüri Talvet
A Call for Cultural Symbiosis, by Jüri Talvet, trans. with the author
City of Ash, by Eugenijus Ališanka, trans. with the author

ARTIST CATALOGS

Jason Pollen
Kyoung Ae Cho

THEORY AND CRITICISM

Wild and Whirling Words: A Poetic Conversation *
As Easy As Lying: Essays on Poetry *
Understanding William H. Gass
Understanding W. S. Merwin
Spirits Hovering Over the Ashes: Legacies of Postmodern Theory
Morte d'Author: An Autopsy

*Also published by Etruscan Press.

—— GOD BLESS ——

A Political/Poetic Discourse Mediated by

H. L. Hix

For Dixie and Queenie:
You see that a state Kick has driven me to!

"If you do not tell the truth to the American
people, there is going to be a consequence."
— George W. Bush
14 August 2002

Etruscan Press
84 West South Street
Wilkes-Barre, PA 18766
www.etruscanpress.org

Printed in the United States of America.

Cover painting "Deconstruction of King George 3" by Robert Carioscia. Book design by Jesse R. Ewing, The Monkey Mensch Gang.

The text of this book is set in Baskerville.

LIBRARY OF CONGRESS CATALOGING-IN-PUBLICATION DATA
Hix, H. L.
   God bless : a political/poetic discourse / mediated by H. L. Hix
   p.   cm.
   ISBN-13: 978-0-9745995-7-1
   ISBN-10: 0-9745995-7-3

   1. Political poetry. I. Title

PS3558.I88G63 2007
811'.54   QBI07-600070

ACKNOWLEDGMENTS

I am grateful to Kris DeForest for heroic research assistance, and to the editors of *The Boston Review*, *Green Mountains Review*, *Madhatters Review*, *Provincetown Arts*, and *Unsplendid* for previous publication of parts of this project.

The two opening epigraphs come from, respectively, George W. Bush in a "press availability" on 2 January 2003, and the King James Version of words attributed to Jesus at Matthew 11:15. The closing epigraph comes from George W. Bush in a 20 November 2002 press conference.

TABLE OF CONTENTS

POEMS

January 2001   13

February 2001   14

Interleaf   15

May 2001   16

July 2001   18

Interleaf   20

September 2001   21

November 2001   22

Interleaf   23

January 2002   24

April 2002   25

Interleaf   27

June 2002   28

July 2002   30

Interleaf   33

September 2002   34

October 2002   36

Interleaf   38

March 2003   39

April 2003   40

Interleaf   43

May 2003   44

July 2003   45

Interleaf   46

September 2003   48

October 2003   49

Interleaf   50

January 2004   51

February 2004   52

Interleaf   54

May 2004   55

August 2004   57

Interleaf   59

September 2004   60

November 2004   61

Interleaf   63

January 2005   64

INTERVIEWS

Philip Brady interviews H. L. Hix   69

M. Javad Zarif   79

Asma Afsaruddin   90

Peter Bergen   103

Paul Woodruff   111

Juliana Spahr   118

Mary Habeck   124

Ross Talarico   135

Richard Kearney   141

Miriam Cooke   153

Pheng Cheah   161

Works Cited   171

Contributors   173

A NOTE ON THE POEMS

The poems designated by a month are constructed entirely
of passages from speeches, executive orders, and other public
statements of George W. Bush. All passages in a given poem were
spoken by Bush during the month that appears as the poem's title,
and all are quoted verbatim, as they appear on the official White
House web site, www.whitehouse.gov. Ellipses signal omissions
within an otherwise continuous excerpt, but no attempt is made to
signal where one quoted passage joins another: the selection and
juxtaposition of the passages is entirely my own.

The "interleaves" respond to (usually by imitating an argument
from) the letters, speeches, and other discourses of Osama bin
Laden. Only the italicized passages are direct quotations from bin
Laden. My source for bin Laden's discourses was *Messages to the
World: The Statements of Osama bin Laden*, ed. Bruce Lawrence, trans.
James Howarth (New York: Verso, 2005).

Can you envision me sitting here, on the rock,
writing some poetry?

He that hath ears to hear, let him hear.

January 2001

The principle here is a basic one:
children must be tested every year.
My administration has no greater
priority than education.
I will work to build a single nation
of justice and opportunity.
The dogs seem to have adjusted. I worry:
one year, you may test and everything is fine.
I'm going to protect that privilege.
Every child must be taught these principles:
we will build our defenses beyond challenge,
we'll see how that affects possible arms talks.
In four years, you measure again,
and all of a sudden something isn't fine.

February 2001

The United States will handle
its responsibilities to keep the peace
by recognizing there are people
struggling to get in the middle class.
We need more power, pure and simple,
to make...the world a more peaceful place.

We live in a dangerous world, a world
that sometimes does not share American values.
There are new threats ... that require theater-based
antiballistic missile systems.
We've got a shortage of gas and a growing demand,
we have a duty to watch for warning signs.

I hope it worries members of Congress.
I think our nation needs to be wary.
Our first response to evil must be justice.
God bless the United States military.
My plan unlocks the door to the middle class.
My job is to lead. Well, God bless, obviously.

Interleaf

No one is *not* engaged in this struggle.
Infidels make religious choice financial,
but the martyrs make their faith physical.

Afraid to make their conflicts physical,
America is not fit for a struggle:
their only unity is financial.

Strike America's heart, the financial,
and its swift collapse will be physical.
It will fall after the merest struggle.

So the struggle is both financial and physical.

May 2001

To help Americans . . . cope with rising energy
prices, we need to go find new supply.
But I believe . . . we can not only find new product,
I also say we need to build more refining capacity.
Our ability to deliver gas to consumers
is crucial to . . . peace and prosperity.

We have an opportunity to build an enduring prosperity
by recognizing the problem and by expediting energy
development. That is positive news for U.S. consumers.
Our efforts are guided by a simple test: Will any action increase
          supply?
Our nation must expand refining capacity.
Otherwise, when you transport refined product

from far distances, it doesn't help us . . . store the product.
To build freedom in the world . . . and enduring prosperity,
we need more refining capacity
in America, folks. We have had no energy
policy. We must also increase supply:
it's in the consumer's

interests. On behalf of the American consumer,
we need more electricity wires carrying product,
an abundant, affordable energy supply
integral to our country's prosperity.
I'm going to tell the truth when it comes to energy:
we need more refining capacity.

Our refineries are gasping at 96 percent of capacity.
We've set aside $100 billion to help consumers
with high energy
prices. When the price of refined product
goes up, our nation must seek purposes beyond prosperity,
but we darn sure have to do a better job of finding more supply.

My plan . . . will make the investments necessary to expand supply,
by increasing capacity.
To stimulate trade, to develop prosperity,
there needs to be money in the pockets of our consumers.
We need to understand we need to move more product.
We're going to lead the world when it comes to energy.

The quicker supply gets on, the easier it's going to be for the
   consumers,
modernizing the capacity to move . . . products.
Our prosperity agenda makes a priority of energy.

July 2001

I'm committing this nation to a more peaceful world.
America . . . needs your help by you all living good.
Tolerance is the defining issue for our world.
       We're going to keep the pressure on Iraq.

Our nation has always been guided by a moral compass.
Conquering poverty creates new customers:
it's a defense, as opposed to relying on peace.
       We're going to keep the pressure on Iraq.

Cultures and hope change as a result of our compassion.
You're free to worship any religion,
But the market ought to make that decision.
       We're going to keep the pressure on Iraq.

The next 10 years will bring more forms of crime . . .
from beyond our borders and within them.
We will pursue a world of tolerance and freedom.
       We're going to keep the pressure on Iraq.

We should not fear faith in our society.
There are new threats in the 21st century,
some things that are unacceptable to me.
       We're going to keep the pressure on Iraq.

I understand politics pretty well,
the power of truth to overcome evil.
To rid the world of blackmail, terrorist blackmail,
       we're going to keep the pressure on Iraq.

I'm very open-minded on the subject.
We're more than willing to cooperate.
I thought that our military should be used to fight.
       We're going to keep the pressure on Iraq.

I'm a proud man to be the nation,
to kind of continue our general conversation.
When I'm ready, I will lay out my decision:
     we're going to keep the pressure on Iraq.

Interleaf

They have no authority over Muslims,
these apostate rulers who defy God.

Freedom cannot be the highest aim
of a people who would obey God.

Neither can peace be the highest aim
of a people who would obey God.

We do not seek the democracy
you would impose. We are ruled by God.

We are not bound to submit to you.
We submit first and only to God.

We do not fear death. We do not fear war.
We do not fear you. We fear only God.

Bin Laden does not defer to you.
Bin Laden defers only to God.

September 2001

Our country will . . . not be cowed by terrorists,
by people who don't share the same values we share.
Those responsible for these cowardly acts
hate our values; they hate what America stands for.
We can't let terrorism dictate our course of action.
We're a nation that has fabulous values:
as a nation of good folks, we're going to hunt them down,
and we're going to find them, and . . . bring them to justice.
Either you are with us, or you are with the terrorists.
They're flat evil. They have no justification.
There is universal support for what we intend.
Americans are asking: What is expected of us?
I ask you to live your lives, and hug your children.
Go back to work. Get down to Disney World.

November 2001

Our enemies are resourceful, and they are incredibly ruthless.
Our war that we now fight is against terror and evil.

Our enemies have brought only misery and terror.
But we will prevail. We will win. Good will overcome evil.

Our enemies have threatened other acts of terror.
We know that we're fighting evil.

We face an enemy . . . the likes of which we've never seen before.
We're a nation that will not be affected by terror and evil.

We fight an enemy who hides in caves.
The only thing I know certain about him is that he's evil.

This new enemy seeks to destroy our freedom and impose its views.
I view this as a fight between good and evil.

Our enemies . . . have no conscience. They have no mercy.
There is one universal law, and that's terrorism is evil.

The enemy has declared war on us.
I've got something to say about . . . our fight against evil.

This enemy will be defeated because this nation is strong.
Today, we are taking another step in our fight against evil.

We face enemies that hate not our policies, but our existence.
But I'm confident of the outcome. I believe good triumphs over evil.

Interleaf

Are human beings free only in the U.S.?
Can it alone retaliate against injustice?
As you violate our security, so we violate yours.

Manhattan was not the first atrocity.
Lebanon 1982: third fleet, Israelis.
We have been fighting you because we *are free.*

Deceiving yourself about the real reasons
for one disaster only invites a second.
Does a crocodile understand anything other than weapons?

Again and again he claims to know our reason,
and tells you we attacked because we hate freedom.
Perhaps he can tell us why we did not attack Sweden.

January 2002

I will not wait on events, while dangers gather.
These evil ones still want to hit us.
The enemy still lurks out there.
These are facts, not theories.
We'll get 'em. We're going to get 'em.
Our nation must invest in procurement accounts.
I can't tell you how proud I am
of our commitment to values.
Fight on, America. I love you.
Our first priority is to the military
when it comes to the defense of our great land,
but there are some other things you can do:
find somebody who is shut-in, and say,
I'd like to just love you for a second.

April 2002

There is a lot of issues facing us.
We must continue to press forward to peace.
Let the statisticians talk about the numbers.
       I deal with reality every day.

Generations will look back at us,
and I believe they're going to say, thanks.
We've got to act on behalf of the little ones.
       I deal with reality every day.

So long as there is terrorists, we need to find them.
My focus is going to be defending freedom.
There's been some threats recently by Saddam.
       I deal with reality every day.

What went through the mind of the evil people?
We will hold Saddam Hussein accountable.
The policy of my government is . . . removal.
       I deal with reality every day.

You know my opinion about Saddam.
The world would be better off without him.
I will lead this nation to defend freedom.
       I deal with reality every day.

Our intelligence . . . is better than it's ever been.
Don't . . . worry about this administration.
I've never been more upbeat about a nation.
       I deal with reality every day.

Our energy comes from other countries.
And some of those countries don't like us.
Some of them aren't our friends.
       I deal with reality every day.

We've got an enemy that hates us,
that is nothing but cold-blooded killers.
No nation can negotiate with terrorists.
       I deal with reality every day.

There are still a lot of them out there.
They are going to try to hurt us; they are.
The people we're dealing with are cold-blooded killers.
       I deal with reality every day.

I believe—that out of this evil will come peace.
I firmly believe that God is on the side of justice.
I've got a vision for the Middle East.
       I deal with reality every day.

About the enemy, I believe they're evil.
I mean, these were barbaric, backward people.
I think regime change sounds a lot more civil.
       I deal with reality every day.

Nations . . . are going to develop these weapons.
We've got to secure this civilization.
You're a smart guy. Read between the lines.
       I deal with reality every day.

Interleaf

How angry America gets
when it attacks people and those people resist!
All religions allow self-defense.
Not only Muslims, but Christians, Jews, even Buddhists
may defend themselves. The Koreans
defended themselves, as did the Vietnamese.
So to answer your question, yes,
I have incited to *jihad* all my Muslim brothers.
May God accept as martyrs
all who have died or been captured practicing resistance.
Khaled al-Sa'id, Abd al-Aziz,
Maslah al-Shamrani, Riyadh al-Hajiri: theirs
is the honor the rest of us missed,
to die for following God's decrees, killing Crusaders.
Other allegations are false,
but incitement to *jihad*, that I have practiced for years
and will keep practicing, by God's grace.

June 2002

In this new war, against this shadowy enemy,
I'm going to talk about homeland security.
In order to make sure this economy
is strong, all of us involved in public policy
will use money, the taxpayers' money,
to do some more in Washington, D.C.

The culture is shifting in Washington, D.C.
because we face a formidable enemy.
It doesn't require a lot of money
for them to operate. Our security
will require the best intelligence, the right public policy.
I understand the need to have a hopeful economy.

I've got confidence in our economy.
There is fiscal discipline in Washington, D.C.
We need an energy policy
because we fight a shadowy enemy.
I'm worried about economic security.
When it comes to spending money,

spending your money,
when it comes to our economy,
when we talk about homeland security,
there's a lot of turf in Washington, D.C.
We must take the battle to the enemy.
This has been an incredibly successful . . . social policy.

I will drive public policy and foreign policy
to let people keep more of their own money.
To defend freedom, and to defeat this enemy
will require a vibrant economy.
There's going to be some budget struggles in Washington, D.C.
as we make progress towards security.

I called for the Department of Homeland Security.
The Department would set national policy.
That's just typical Washington, D.C.
I want to thank you for contributing your money.
I worry about our economy,
and now we're facing a new kind of enemy.

We will bring security to our people and justice to our enemies.
Our economy is strong; we've got the right fiscal policy.
We set aside money here in Washington, D.C.

July 2002

There is no wealth without character.
As we prepare our military
the important thing is to restore
confidence to the economy.

To be a patriotic American
we must love our neighbor.
These people, . . . they're poor, and they're downtrodden.
There is no wealth without character.

Help a neighbor in need. I do.
To be a patriotic American
we take lives when we have to.
We worry about weapons of mass destruction.

We take lives when we have to.
We're going to chase them down one by one,
that's what we're going to do,
is to hunt these cold-blooded killers down.

We're a compassionate nation,
and so we're on the hunt.
We're going to chase them down one by one
so long as I'm the President.

Out of the evil . . . will come great good
because I'm the President.
Terrorism is fueled by boundless hatred.
We will offer a fabulous product.

We value life; the enemy hates life.
That's what we're going to do,
defend civilization itself.
This isn't a—the type of war we're all used to.

We do what we do for peace.
It's just a different type of war.
Let me tell you what I think the bill says:
there is no wealth without character.

We need men and women . . . who know the difference
between ambition and destructive greed.
I think that's an important nuance.
Out of the evil . . . will come great good.

We still feel like we're under attack.
The war goes on. We're making progress.
This economy is coming back.
We do what we do for peace.

And so we're on the hunt:
the largest increase in our defense spending
since Ronald Reagan was the President,
to hold people accountable for killing.

We're a compassionate nation,
and the results are better as a result.
You know what's going to happen?
So long as I'm the President

the world will be safer and more peaceful.
You can imagine what that is like,
trying to hold somebody accountable.
We still feel like we're under attack.

I do firmly believe . . . a regime change,
that's what we're going to do.
Not because we seek revenge:
we owe it to history, we owe it to

our children and our grandchildren
to hold somebody accountable,
to hunt these cold-blooded killers down.
It's a great country, because we're great people.

We're prepared for any enemy.
We're not going to worry about process.
The important thing is . . . the economy.
We do what we do for peace.

Interleaf

The Crusader world has agreed to devour us.
The world conspires to consume the Islamic world.
The nations have rallied together against us.

God's book warns against befriending the infidels:
read the exegesis of ibn Kathir.
The Crusader world has agreed to devour us.

"Do not take the Jews and Christians as friends."
This command from God Almighty could not be more clear.
The nations have rallied together against us.

It is our meeting with God for which *jihad* prepares.
Life in this world is an illusory pleasure.
The Crusader world has agreed to devour us.

We must realize how few are this world's rewards,
that the next world's are more permanent and better.
The nations have rallied together against us.

Arab leaders are fools to seek Christian allies;
except in God there is no strength or power.
The Crusader world has agreed to devour us.
The nations have rallied together against us.

September 2002

I'm here to talk about the greatness of this country.
Why would you hate America?
We didn't do anything to anybody.
       We believe in peace.

At Guantánamo, all are being treated humanely,
to the extent appropriate
and consistent with military necessity.
       We love and long for peace.

I don't trust Iraq, and neither should the free world.
There are al Qaeda killers
lurking in the neighborhood.
       I want there to be peace.

Saddam Hussein's regime
is a grave and gathering danger.
He is a significant problem.
       My desire is to achieve peace.

Some up here don't get it, see.
He basically told the United Nations,
your deal don't mean anything to me.
       I long for peace.

One thing is for certain.
I don't know what more evidence we need.
He holds weapons of mass destruction.
       Our job is to keep the peace.

It's time with us to deal with Saddam Hussein.
We must anticipate.
He's a man who has got weapons of mass destruction.
       I want there to be a peaceful world.

The Iraqi regime
possesses biological and chemical weapons.
You can't distinguish between al Qaeda and Saddam.
      My goal is peace. I long for peace.

Saddam Hussein has side-stepped, crawfished, wheedled.
I don't appreciate it one bit.
He is stiffing the world.
      I'm willing to give peace a chance.

It's a different kind of war.
It's a different kind of hater than we're used to.
He has invaded two countries before.
      We're a peaceful people.

This is a man who continually lies.
This is a man who does not know the truth.
This is a man who is a threat to peace.
      The world will thank the United States.

This great country is responding to
al Qaeda and Saddam Hussein.
I can't distinguish between the two.
      To keep the peace, you've got to . . . use force.

In Iraq, they don't believe in liberty.
They think they can outwit us, but they can't.
Haters don't—can't see.
      We love peace and we love freedom.

I'm talking about Iraq.
They should cherish American values.
I want you to know that behind the rhetoric
      is a deep desire for peace.

October 2002

I want to explain to you about Saddam Hussein, just quickly, if I
      might.
The facts and the history of Iraq are pretty clear to me.
If we know Saddam Hussein has dangerous weapons today—
and we do—does it make any sense for the world to wait?

We never seek to impose our culture or our form of government.
We just want to live under those universal values, God-given
      values.
We've got to be clear-eyed about the new dangers we face.
I don't view this as a political discourse or a political debate.

The dictator of Iraq is a student of Stalin.
America is a friend to the people of Iraq.
We've got to button up our homeland. And, therefore, I will
      continue to speak
clearly about good and evil. It starts with upholding doctrine.

Some worry that a change of leadership in Iraq could create
      instability
and make the situation worse. The situation could hardly get
      worse.
We're liberators in this case, and we'll always be liberators.
Our country never has the intention of conquering anybody.

We have no plans to use our military until—unless we need to.
The Iraqi people . . . will be the first to benefit.
There is universal agreement that Saddam Hussein poses a serious
      threat.
Our job is to make the world a more peaceful place. That's what
      we've got to do.

Let me explain to you why this country is determined.
If we hold our values, God-given values, here's what's going to
      happen:

the long captivity of Iraq will end, and an era of new hope will begin.

To fight evil, all you've got to do is do some good.

Interleaf

We are determined, with God's will,
      to continue our struggle,
to build on what we've done before
      against the merchants of war,
but I make this peace proposal,
      a commitment to cease all
operations against any state
      that will keep a pledge not
to attack Muslims or intervene
      in our affairs—even
America. We can reaffirm
      this peace with each new term
of office for its president,
      upon mutual consent.
It will take effect upon departure
      of the last soldier
from Islamic lands. If you choose war,
      we stand ready for war,
if you choose peace, we will keep the peace.
      Now you must make your choice.
To save your own blood is in your powers:
      simply stop spilling ours.

March 2003

America made a decision:
We will not wait for our enemies to strike
before we act against them. Saddam Hussein
is a threat. We're dealing with Iraq.

He has weapons of mass destruction.
We're not going to wait until he does attack.
We . . . don't need anybody's permission.
Our mission is clear, to disarm Iraq.

We will stay on task, my fellow citizens.
It's an old Texas expression, show your cards.
Iraq will be free. One of the big concerns
early on was the Southern oil fields.

I've thought long and hard about the use
of troops. I think about it all the time.
We will . . . protect Iraq's natural resources
from sabotage by a dying regime.

We are coming to bring you food and medicine
and a better life. Do not destroy oil wells.
Our cause is just. We have no ambition.
We have secured more than 600 oil wells.

Our mission is very clear: disarmament.
God will bless and receive each of the fallen.
Pray for peace. In terms of the dollar amount,
well, we'll let you know here pretty soon.

April 2003

We honor their service to America and we pray
their families will receive God's comfort and God's grace.

We pray for their speedy and safe return.
May God bless our country and all who defend her.

We pray for those families who mourn the loss of life.
We believe freedom is—is a gift from the Almighty God.

We pray that they are alive, because if they are, we'll find them.
We know that freedom is the gift of God to all mankind.

We pray that they, too, will be safe and free one of these days.
God bless our country.

A lot of them told me that they had been sustained by prayer.
May God bless you.

They told me that they felt like prayers had been answered.
And may God continue to bless America.

Prayer is powerful.
God bless you all.

One of the great things about this country is a lot of people pray.
Passover reminds individuals of God's faithfulness.

I know a lot of people are praying for the families of those who
        grieve.
I thank God for their lives.

America mourns those who have been called home, and we pray
that their families will find God's comfort and God's grace.

Gather at the Seder table to eat special foods, offer prayers, and
     sing songs.
Freedom is God's gift to each and every person of the world.

This Easter season, join me in praying for peace, wisdom, and
     resolve.
This country believes that freedom is God's gift.

Our grateful nation remembers them in prayer.
May God bless you, and may God bless America.

As a nation, we continue to pray for all who serve in our military.
Freedom is God's gift to every person in every nation.

We also pray for those who have lost people they love in this war.
May God continue to bless the United States of America.

We prayed for peace and for strength,
and for God's promise of freedom for the oppressed.

I want to thank you all for your prayers,
supreme demonstrations of God's mercy, faithfulness, and
     redemption.

We are a Nation whose people turn to prayer.
Thank you all. God bless.

In prayer, we share the universal desire to speak and listen
to our Maker and to seek the plans He has for our lives.

Prayer will not make our path easy, yet prayer can give us strength.
Thank God for our Nation's many blessings.

We pray that their loved ones
will receive God's comfort and grace.

Join me in praying for the strength to meet the challenges before us.
We are grateful for our freedom, for God's love, mercy, and
     forgiveness.

I ask the citizens of our Nation to pray.
May God bless what you do.

Interleaf

Don't let their numbers frighten you,
for their hearts are empty.

Don't let their weapons frighten you,
for their faith is empty.

Don't let their threats intimidate you,
for they have not the will
to carry them out.

Don't let their lies deceive you;
their self-deception is your weapon.

Don't let their money persuade you;
it was printed with your brothers' blood.

Don't let their cynicism infect you;
money has no true friends,
but looks out only for itself.

Don't let their blasphemy corrupt you;
they think even God belongs to them.

Don't let their greed corrupt you;
God is not impressed by possessions.

Don't let their numbers frighten you,
for their hearts are empty.

May 2003

My fellow Americans:
the tyrant has fallen, and Iraq is free.
Combat operations
in Iraq have ended. We're an ownership society.
That's what we want.
We want our citizens to be wealthier.
We will hunt
the terrorists in every dark corner
of the earth.
We believe in peace, in keeping the peace.
The world will see the truth.
Democracy can work. You see, we hold values
dear to our heart.
Saddam Hussein had weapons of mass destruction.
Peace requires the defeat
of terror. This is a peaceful nation.
The Senate
passed a bill to help ease the suffering on
the African continent.
Things aren't going as good as they can.
When we feel
like sharing the information with you,
we will.
We'll find them. We have a lot of work to do.
The terrorists,
you can't talk to them, you can't negotiate.
The United States
will bring peace. The initiative I've laid out
is beginning to make sense.
Our actions have been focused . . . and proportionate
to the offense.
The world is more peaceful, there's absolutely no doubt.

July 2003

Our country made the right decision.
We're realists in this administration.
I believe God has called us into action.

First of all, the war on terror goes on.
The first value is, we're all God's children.
Our country made the right decision.

I am confident that Saddam Hussein
had a weapons of mass destruction
program. God has called us into action.

Nobody likes to have the whistle blown.
I think the intelligence I get is darn
good. Our country made the right decision.

I did the right thing. A free Iraq will mean
a peaceful world. My answer is, bring them on.
I believe God has called us into action.

The al Qaeda terrorists still threaten
our country, but they're on the run.
Our country made the right decision.
I believe God has called us into action.

Interleaf

To attentive observers it may seem
that *we and the White House are on the same team,*

bleeding the American economy
to what will soon enough be bankruptcy,

as the mujahidin in Afghanistan
drained to its death the Soviet Union.

It should be plain to Americans
that, though all countries supported inspection,

none of them urged, and few now sanction,
this *groundless war with unknown repercussions,*

but Bush *put his own private interests
ahead of American public interest,*

paying himself and his administration
with no-bid contracts to Halliburton.

*The war went ahead and many were killed.
The American economy bled.*

Iraquis he has killed by the thousands,
but also American youth. Bush's hands

bear the blood of all these casualties,
who died making business for his companies.

Al Qaeda spent five hundred thousand on
what cost America five hundred billion;

Bush and his cronies continue to siphon
billions into pointless occupation.

What al Qaeda did and what Bush chose:
it is the American people who lose.

September 2003

Laura sends her love. We're a strong country,
and we use our strength to defend the peace.
I'm interested in solving problems quickly.

I have proposed a good plan to the Congress:
a strategy in Iraq and a mission,
the work that history has set before us.

I have laid out a comprehensive plan.
I know there's talk about the deficit,
first of all, the $87 billion,

but the $87 billion is worth it.
We have carried the fight to the enemy.
With these people, you can't negotiate.

The signs are . . . good about our economy.
Peaceful Iraq will save this country money.

October 2003

We now see our enemy clearly.
We'll fight them with everything we got.
We believe in decency.
The terrorists continue to plot.
We don't torture people in America.
I don't care what you read about.
They know no rules, they know no law,
but we're incredibly compassionate.
America's ideology
is based upon compassion
and decency and justice.
Nearly every day
we're launching swift precision
raids against the enemies of peace.

Interleaf

That your methods reveal your cowardice
does not restore our women and children
or lessen our suffering over their loss.
What shall we call deaths by enforced starvation?
Is murder only murder as explosion?
Someone in the darkness has to call it night.
Someone has to ask the obvious question:
If self-defense is terrorism, what is legitimate?

That your people believe your cynical lies
doesn't make them true, nor does repetition;
does not make those bombed at evening prayers
in the mosque at Khost less dead, less civilian.
Group our men, call us al Qaeda, Taliban;
are our children any less innocent
than yours, that their deaths should not cause us to mourn?
If self-defense is terrorism, what is legitimate?

Even confrontation with the evidence
cannot overcome your repression.
You substitute denial for conscience.
Three civilians murdered in Afghanistan
as collateral for each American
in the towers. Videotaped, the incident
of Muhammad al Durreh gunned down.
If self-defense is terrorism, what is legitimate?

Riyadh for Iraq, Kashmir, Lebanon.
Cole for occupying our holiest site.
Manhattan for Burma and Palestine.
If self-defense is terrorism, what is legitimate?

January 2004

This is a common-sense plan.
It makes eminent sense.
It puts money in circulation.
That's how the economy works.
   It seems like to me it makes sense.

My budget nearly triples
homeland security spending
over 2001 levels.
Freedom is happening.
   It seems like to me it makes sense.

I quit drinking because
I changed my heart. I guess I was
a one-man faith-based program.
Keep the peace by spreading freedom.
   It seems like to me it makes sense.

It is a plan that recognizes
reality in a common-sense way.
Look at the facts. And the fact is
Iraq is more free every day.
   It seems like to me it makes sense.

A dangerous man, Saddam:
he had deep hatred in his heart
for people who love freedom.
We live in a time set apart.
   It seems like to me it makes sense.

Now we're marching to peace.
Now, things are looking pretty good.
Stay on the offensive: it's
in the interest of the neighborhood.
   It seems like to me it makes sense.

February 2004

Every American is threatened.
        Americans always do what is right.
I'm not going to change my opinion.
Every American is threatened.
Look, we need money here. I understand
        my job as your President.
Every American is threatened.
        Americans always do what is right.

We're good at things. By our actions
        we have shown what kind of nation we are.
America believes in elections.
We're good at things. By our actions
terrorists have learned the meaning of justice.
        I made the tough decision to go to war.
We're good at things. By our actions
        we have shown what kind of nation we are.

And I work for free societies
        because I believe in people.
We need money to meet priorities,
and I work for free societies.
I led. Now we're marching to peace.
        Now the world is more peaceful.
And I work for free societies
        because I believe in people.

My attitude is, there's been tremendous
        death and destruction because killers kill.
We . . . continue to open up markets.
My attitude is, there's been tremendous
liberation. We're doing things more wise.
        They are ruthless, and they are resourceful.
My attitude is, there's been tremendous
        death and destruction because killers kill.

We've got kind of a gap in the pipeline,
      but we dealt with it straightforward.
Democratic reform must come from within.
We've got kind of a gap in the pipeline,
but we acted, here in Washington,
      and that changed us, it really did.
We've got kind of a gap in the pipeline,
      but we dealt with it straightforward.

Interleaf

You demand that Americans taken
as prisoners of war be treated well,
by terms of the Geneva Convention,
but you imprison us without trial,
without recourse, without stated cause.
You torture us at Guantánamo Bay.
You accept our surrender at Qunduz,
only to murder us along the way
to prison in Jangi by the hundreds,
packed despite this heat into a boxcar
to die of suffocation and thirst.
You treat your chickens and cattle better.
You like to impose principles and values,
but follow them yourself only when you choose.

May 2004

Let me talk about America.
See, we're good at things here in America.

I envision a new culture and it's happening,
not because of me, but because of America.

Each of us is responsible for loving our neighbor
like we'd like to be loved yourself. America

is marching to war. There's still an enemy
that would like to strike America.

They won't intimidate us. They're not
going to frighten us. This is America.

Our message is positive and optimistic:
to protect the American people

from an enemy which is cold-blooded.
But the best way to protect America

is to stay on the offensive and bring
these killers to justice. America

is leading the way. My job is to rally
the compassion of America.

There is no cave or hole deep enough
to hide from American justice.

America won't relent. That's the spirit
of a compassionate, better America.

I can't tell you how proud I am of Laura.
She loves the children of America.

The true strength of the country is the hearts
and souls of the American people.

I have a plan to make sure prosperity
reaches every corner of America.

We've got a positive vision for everybody.
The security and prosperity of America

increases the demand for energy.
I will defend the security of America,

whatever it takes. May God bless you all.
May God continue to bless America.

August 2004

Lesson one is, there's an enemy
out there. That's why I'm running with Dick Cheney.
We stand for institutions like marriage and family,
which are the foundations of our society,
and that stands in stark contrast to the enemy.
We will lead the world with confidence and moral clarity.
You'll hear me talk about our military
later on and our economy.
In Iraq and Afghanistan we need more money
for our troops, $87 billion more money.
These funds are necessary
to support Operation Iraqi
Freedom. It's our most solemn duty:
ammunition, fuel, spare parts for our military.
This money will buy more armored Humvees.
I think it's a wise use of taxpayers' money,
being on the offense against an enemy.
By serving the ideal of liberty,
we're spreading peace. George Bush and Dick Cheney
are what's best for this country.
Our efforts are unified in priority
and purpose, because there's an enemy
that still wants to harm us. That's the reality
of the world. We spend the people's money
to defeat the terrorist enemy.
It's now providing more energy
for us. The Iraqi people are free.
I will never relent in chasing down the enemy.
These people don't like freedom. You know why?
Because it clashes with their ideology.
And it's really important that we never forget that reality.
We regulate a lot here in Washington, D.C.
We have a solemn responsibility
for the defense of the traditional family.
It's a war in which the enemy is an enemy
that has a dark ideology.

My most solemn duty is to protect our country.
America must take threats seriously.
Deep in my soul, I know that there's an enemy
that lurks and still hates us. We're a free country.
We believe in freedom and liberty.
We got plenty of capability
of dealing with justice. We support free
and fair trade. We're facing an enemy
which has no heart, no compassion. If somebody
has done some wrong in our military,
we'll take care of it. Sound policy
can help unleash the initiative and talent of free
people. We believe in human dignity:
that's the core of our philosophy.
The use of force in Iraq was necessary,
and the $87 billion was necessary
to make our country safer, to make our economy
stronger. Saddam Hussein had the capability
to make weapons. He was a source of great instability,
but for the sake of energy security, Dick Cheney
is solid as a rock. Freedom is the Almighty
God's gift. We must engage the enemy.
We're doing wise things with our military.
We're getting the job done in Washington, D.C.
When you get more products coming into the country,
you can shop. That ought to be the first priority
of any President. That's good trade policy.
Pray for me and Laura and our family.
We're going to do what's necessary
to protect this country. The enemy
attacked us and we got to respond. You see,
when we acted to protect our own security,
we promised to help deliver them from tyranny,
to restore their sovereignty,
and to help set them on the road to liberty.
We've got a fantastic military.
I made the decision to go after the enemy.
May God continue to bless our great country.

Interleaf

Wherever we look, we see the US
as the leader of terrorism and crime.
If a Palestinian, if any Muslim
retaliates, they condemn and attack us.

Gerry Adams can visit the White House;
Ramzi Yousef, they imprison and condemn.
Wherever we look, we see the US
as the leader of terrorism and crime.

Who stations troops at all points of the compass?
Which country has dropped an atomic bomb?
Kabul, Baghdad: who occupies whom?
Who is desperate for whose resources?
Wherever we look, we see the US
as the leader of terrorism and crime.

September 2004

We're getting the job done.
We have overcome a recession.
It was the right decision
to go into Iraq. Saddam Hussein
and the Taliban.
Weapons of mass destruction.

Dick Cheney is a solid citizen.
We have got a plan:
fuel and spare parts and ammunition.
$87 billion.
A struggle of historic proportion.
Weapons of mass destruction.

To everything we know there is a season.
People who want a job can find one.
Our mission in Afghanistan
and Iraq is clear: comfort in
God's promise, which has never been broken.
Weapons of mass destruction.

November 2004

No President should ever try to impose religion,
but I'm the kind of fellow who does what I think is right.

Freedom is the Almighty God's gift.
Thank you all for coming. God bless.
Freedom is the Almighty God's gift.
God bless and thanks for coming.
Freedom is the Almighty God's gift.
God bless, and thank you for coming.
Freedom is the Almighty God's gift.
Thanks for coming. God bless.
Freedom is the Almighty God's gift.
Freedom is the Almighty God's gift.
Thank you for coming. God bless.
God bless you, and may God bless America.
My first reaction is, God bless his soul.
And so we wish our troops all the best and Godspeed.
It is a time to think of the less fortunate, and to share God's gifts
        with those in need.
Freedom is the Almighty God's gift.
We will always protect the most basic human freedom—the
        freedom to worship the Almighty God.
We share a belief in God's justice.
May God bless you all.
With the consent of the Senate, God's help and the support of my
        family, I will do my best.
May God bless our veterans and their families, and may God
        continue to bless our great nation.
Human dignity is the gift of God.
We are a nation founded by men and women who deeply felt their
        dependence on God and always gave Him thanks and
        praise.
May God bless you all, and may God continue to bless our country.
God bless you.
God bless.

We gather this week with the people we love to give thanks to God
for the blessings in our lives.

All of these things, and life itself, come from the Almighty God.

The Pilgrims celebrated a harvest feast to thank God.

Americans have gathered with family and friends and given thanks
to God for our blessings.

We thank God for His blessings and ask Him to continue to guide
and watch over our Nation.

We offer thanks and praise to the provider of all these gifts,
Almighty God.

The pilgrims set aside time to thank God.

Interleaf

It is in the interests of Americans
no less than of Arabs to stop those
who shed their own people's blood without remorse
to serve their narrow personal interests.
The war in Iraq is making billions
for those who manufacture weapons
and for other large corporations—
Halliburton and its susidiaries—
with ties to those who make the decisions.
This is a war begun by the CEOs
of those who receive the no-bid contracts,
the same who help to privatize defense.
Which kills more Americans, our attacks or
the collusion of these merchants of war?

January 2005

America will not impose our own style of government.
Freedom, by its nature, must be chosen.
It is human choices that move events.
America will not impose our own style of government.
Democracy is a prelude to our enemies' defeat.
America's vital interests and our . . . beliefs are now one.
America will not impose our own style of government.
Freedom, by its nature, must be chosen.

No one has ever accused me of being a poet before, but thank you.

A NOTE ON THE INTERVIEWS

Whatever else they may be doing, the preceding poems imagine into conversation traumatizations of language through which two powerful public figures refused to speak to one another. To lament the tragic consequences of a failure to converse is to solicit conversation, so the poems are here followed by interviews with persons perceived by the poet to have information or perspective that bears on issues raised by the poems. The interviews do not purport to represent all the perspectives needed for a robust conversation, only certain ones the poet considers un- or under-represented in current policymaking; collectively, the interviews do not attempt to complete a conversation, but to extend and enrich one.

Philip Brady's interview of H. L. Hix is presented first; the other interviews were conducted by H. L. Hix, and are presented chronologically.

Philip Brady interviews H. L. Hix
18 February 2007

*This book is unlike anything else you've done. Tell me a little about what
generated the project.*

I've felt in recent years a heightening sense of political obligation
and civic responsibility. Our country has taken a course, especially
in foreign policy, that I find troubling, and that shows up in my
life as a perceived need to apologize to friends overseas when I
correspond with them, and as a growing realization that I've been
a free rider enjoying the benefits of the circumstances I was born
into, without always taking responsibility for their consequences.
This sense that our country is doing worse for itself right now
than in the past has motivated me to try to be a less passive citizen.
The simpler rationale is that my poetry and probably my activities
in general tend to manifest obsessions. I try to follow my obsessions.
At one point I became obsessed with the public discourse of our
current president, and this book came out of that obsession.

*God Bless shares with your previous work a pervasive concern with
exploring the relationship between the form of what you do and the meaning
generated. What are the central issues for you that are being put forward as
you present Bush and bin Laden in this inventive poetic form?*

I'm sure a lot of different issues get raised, and probably in many
ways I am not the best spokesperson for the book, but I think
I would appeal to the often-quoted passage from one of Yeats'
prose works, that "we make of the quarrel with others, rhetoric,
and of the quarrel with ourselves, poetry." This book lets poetry
and rhetoric butt heads, in such a way that there are two kinds
of interrogation going on. The rhetoric of Bush and bin Laden is
interrogating poetry, and the poetry is interrogating the rhetoric of
Bush and bin Laden.

The rhetoric's interrogation of the poetry might be formulated
in such questions as, is it a poem if it puts public political speech

into verse forms? If you cut and paste a campaign speech into the form of a sonnet, lines that end with rhymes in a certain pattern, is that a poem just because it's in the form of a poem? The reverse process, poetry interrogating rhetoric, raises such questions as, can discourse—of whatever sort, rhetoric or poetry—can discourse become truthful if it's originally uttered as a deceptive language use? In other words, can you use words or sentences that were spoken with intent to deceive, can you re-contextualize them in such a way that they become truthful, not necessarily meaning what they were originally meant to mean, but somehow made truthful? This book is an experiment to raise that kind of question, I guess.

From the start, when we passed the first manuscript of God Bless *around among friends of the press, there have been a wide variety of responses, and not all of them positive. One way or the other, people have strong opinions. For instance, some readers ask about the validity of using excerpts from Bush in a world of sound bites where people are often misquoted and made to seem to mean things that they don't intend. When politicians are subjected to that treatment, we usually consider it unethical. Certainly that was a factor in the last election. Wouldn't any politician or public figure be liable to sound ridiculous if their quotes were taken out of context? What distinguishes Bush as your choice of a target over other politicians?*

I'm sure any of us could be made to sound dumb if our words were taken out of context and rearranged, one sentence put into connection with another or only a portion quoted and not the whole thing. We see that happening all the time. Bush was very good at it in his campaigns: partially quoting or misquoting or re-contextualizing passages from his opponent. And we see it in other contexts: book blurbs made from a short passage of a review. Take the sentence "this book could be marvelous if only it were written by another person" and just pull out the word marvelous, surround it by ellipses, add an exclamation point, and you have something entirely different. Language is susceptible to that and consequently we all are susceptible. But I think that this can be done in more or less interesting ways, and that particular kind of thing—the book blurb—seems ultimately less interesting to me.

But I think there are also interesting ways for this to happen. Caricature is an example, through which one sees a face as one has not seen it before, and maybe in a way that is somehow valid or revealing even though it is not "accurate." If I draw a caricature of your face, I'm not trying to replicate your face, I'm trying to draw attention to various features of it, maybe how it's different from other faces and so on. So caricature is one form of distortion that has its own purpose and validity. Satire, if we are talking specifically about linguistic phenomena, is another example. In logic, the reductio ad absurdum, a kind of parody that shows, "this argument looks valid but actually it's not." There are a lot of ways in which something other than full and straight quotation might be, in certain contexts and for certain purposes, interesting and revealing.

But why didn't I write an analogous book when Clinton was in office, or George Bush Sr.? Partly, the accidental fact that the idea never occurred to me. But also because I think there is a real difference in how the presidency is being handled at this moment; how the U.S. is disporting itself in relation to the rest of the world. Different in a way that is not only tied to my particular political views. No one would be surprised to learn that I typically vote for Democrats in preference to Republicans, but I don't think that's the primary issue. I would not have been inclined toward such a project in relation to George Bush Sr., who seems to me to have undertaken the office with a different approach. At least subtler, if not more noble. So, it's not an issue of party affiliation, but some larger thing that might be formulated as a level of cynicism. Bush seems to me to be causing more harm than for example his predecessor, Clinton, in at least a couple of ways. One of them I would call the focus of deception. The most blatant lies that Clinton uttered were about sex, which seems to me to have a very limited relevance to the nation and the world. The sorts of things that are problematic about the Bush administration, such as non-compete bids awarded to companies with which he and others in his administration are closely affiliated, non-compete bids for billions of dollars of taxpayers' money and the decision to go to war to create the need for those non-compete bids, those lies cause the deaths of thousands of people, and have a major impact on millions more. They impact the lives of citizens in a much more important way than do lies about who the President is having sex with.

In addition to the focus of deception is the level of self awareness. It seems to me that Clinton, when he lied, knew he was lying and was doing it on purpose, so when he said, "I did not have sex with that woman," he knew what he had done, and he knew he was lying about it. That might seem to be worse, but there seem to be times when Bush says things that are blatantly false, but that he thinks are true—that he believes in. In terms of consequences to other people, the number of lives they can end for instance, those lies are of much greater magnitude.

Another reader has said that "quoting Bush is not poetry." How do you respond?

Maybe it's not. The book calls itself a "political/poetic discourse," which may be a form of hedging. These things that present themselves as the poems adopt poetic forms, the structures that we normally call poems, but maybe they're not poems. I think that's a question they raise, rather than something I have an answer to or a commitment about. If you decided these are not poems, that's okay with me. I don't so much care whether we call them poems or not, or whether they fulfill whatever criterion we're using to distinguish poems from non-poems. What they're trying to do really doesn't change whether or not we're calling it poetry.

There is a long tradition that we're both very familiar with of political resistance in American poems, with the most recent coalescence around Vietnam. And that tradition seemed to have entered the cultural mainstream, as well as influencing and moving the way poetry is written, the way all art was made. So far at least, the Iraq War doesn't seem to have generated the same level of literary and cultural change. Why haven't writers and artists 'stepped up,' do you think?

I'm sure a lot of factors play into this. This is not the 1960s, and how our government conducts war and how it communicates with the citizenry about that war has changed drastically since Vietnam. Not only because of changes in media but because of what the government learned from Vietnam and from how it communicated about circumstances then. Times are different because of things like the draft. It makes a difference that we have essentially economic criteria for excluding people from or including them in the armed forces. In the 1960s, the draft meant that more people from the more empowered economic classes were at risk of losing their lives in the war. Their families were affected in different ways. So more powerful people were at risk in Vietnam than are at risk in Iraq. For the wealthiest classes, this war has very little significance except in economic terms; it has little to do in personal terms with themselves and their families.

There are other differences, too. I think my generation and those after mine felt less able to have political effects than previous generations did. Some sense that the machine is so big and so efficient that whatever I do is a useless, trivial gesture that has no impact. Though I haven't overcome the perception that there is nothing I can really do, I have begun to ask myself what it would be like if I adopted the fiction of my political effectiveness, the fiction that my vote counts and that my resistance counts. You could reverse things and say okay, I'm also in the generation that saw Eastern European countries gain independence from the Soviet Union. I guess it has just seemed like time to adopt that fiction for myself, and I think I'm not alone. I was very interested to see the kinds of things George Clooney has done with his past couple of films, like the Edward R. Murrow film. I think people are beginning to realize that we've been in a cycle that in its fear and paranoia bears some similarities to the McCarthy era. And there have begun to be signs in popular culture that people are beginning to question, to say hey wait a minute, maybe we've gone too far in this direction and shouldn't we be thinking in some other ways? All of that to say, I guess, that I felt I *had* to write this book.

Another question about the differences between American poetry in its mode of resistance during the Vietnam War, and American poetry now. We've been talking about some of the great poems from that era, like Robert Duncan's

*"Uprising," or Robert Bly's "The Teeth Mother Naked at Last," which bring
new insight and question postures and ways of thinking. "The Teeth Mother
Naked at Last," for example, seems to take it for granted that Johnson lies.
"The ministers lie, the professors lie, the television lies. What are these lies?
They mean that the country wants to die." Then it goes on to say, "Do not
be angry at the president, he is longing to take in his hand the locks of death
hair." Bly seems to be attempting to re-contextualize, or bring new light
to this kind of political activity. This doesn't seem to be the strategy that
you're adopting. How do you see* God Bless *in terms of past traditions of
resistance poetry?*

There are differences in context between Vietnam and this version
of Iraq. Duncan and Bly address a particular type of disillu-
sionment in resisting Johnson. The country has gone from a very
widely revered leader who was tragically and suddenly killed, and
whose recent history had been one that people had trusted and
were happy about: the averting of the Cuban missile crisis, where,
without firing a shot, we succeed in forestalling an enemy, and so
on. It's a very widely and deeply trusted leadership, but the new
leader engaged in policies and practices that were not trusted, and
we saw more clearly that our own motives were dubious, and we
saw that there was a larger dissonance between what we said we
were trying to do—defeat Communism—and what we were really
doing. Plus we just weren't succeeding.

In contrast, Clinton, however he was thought of by different sides,
was not revered by anyone as an honest and noble leader. So the
disillusionment from Clinton to Bush is different, and it seems to
me that that also shows up in terms of the kind of speech being
used. In the '60s you're coming out of a period where the stump
speech remains a kind of common ground of political rhetoric, and
is itself based on the sermon, a widely trusted form of speech, and
the poems that you and I have been talking about as examples of
this type of resistance, the Duncan poem and the Bly poem, are
themselves modeled on the stump speech and the sermon. They're
incantatory, they use the same kinds of rhythms and speech
patterns and so their way of one-upping the misuse of this kind of
rhetoric is to use it more nobly and for better purposes. Our trust of

stump speeches and sermons is far less now than it was forty years ago, and now the kinds of speech that we take for granted, that are all around us, are spin and advertising and the sound bite, and we take those as the normal forms of speech, including political speech, so if you're going to challenge somebody, if you're going to use their speech against them, maybe making the sound bite itself into a mode of resistance is one strategy.

There is another figure who comes up besides George Bush, and that is, of course, Osama bin Laden. As I read God Bless, *bin Laden is a lot saner than George Bush. His arguments are impassioned if dangerous, and don't seem distorted, at least to me. There's no doubt that he opposes us, but he is stripped of the rhetoric you would hear if you were to take quotations from bin Laden, whose speech is full of very heightened religious references as well as references to jihad and anti-Semitic slurs. I'm just wondering why, having dressed George Bush in his most fierce attire, you chose not to adopt the same strategy towards Osama bin Laden?*

I tried! In terms of the history of the project and its process, the Bush poems began first. Then it occurred to me that I really needed the other voice, and I intended to do the same thing, but found that the material didn't lend itself in the same way, so one way of answering your question is that Bush's ways of talking lend themselves to this. He uses short sentences and moves from point to point rapidly, and bin Laden's public statements, at least in translation, have more complex sentences and construct longer thoughts and longer chains of reasoning, so they don't lend themselves in the same way to pulling out a sound bite here and putting it next to this sound bite over here, because they aren't just sound bites, they're actual arguments. Sound or not, kooky or not, hateful or not, it's simply more complex discourse. I tried to replicate the process I was using with Bush, but I couldn't do it.

There's another more principled reason, though, and it has to do with the context. I have to assume that if anyone actually buys this book and reads it, it'll be primarily Americans. Even in my most giddy fantasies of vast readership, sales might extend to Canada, but won't extend into the more predominately Muslim world, so it's primarily a western audience, a western readership that's going to see this, and I think that America has made a terrible, terrible mistake in the response to bin Laden and al Qaeda. It's the mistake of the straw person fallacy, of not hearing the opponent, and if this were the simplest grade school fist fight, the first thing you want to do when you pull the kids into the principal's office is to ask Billy, do you understand why Bobby was mad at you, and Bobby, do you understand why Billy was mad at you? It seems to me that we have been guilty, especially after the trauma of September 11th, of attributing motives, specifically to bin Laden, but also to terrorists generally, and to radical Islam generally. But the motives that Bush attributes to bin Laden are not the motives that bin Laden himself states.

Maybe bin Laden is a liar, but when you're presented with someone who says, here is what I believe, here is why I'm doing what I'm doing, even if they're actions that threaten you—especially if they're actions that threaten you—the first thing to do is understand that person's motivations, if only to better defend yourself. I can better predict what this person's going to do next if I understand his motivations. If I'm a football coach, I'm going to watch a lot of film of the team I'm getting ready to play. Maybe that team uses a 3-4 defense and I use a 4-3. It doesn't matter, I want to understand *their* defense, not the defense I believe in. It seems to me self-destructive to ignore bin Laden's claims, and I think Bush has been a very exaggerated example of this, willfully misattributing motives to bin Laden in ways that hurt us. Never mind whether they do or don't hurt bin Laden. They hurt us. From the start, Bush's decisions were doomed to fail, because he has steadfastly refused to understand the real motivations of the antagonist.

Even the most liberal among us has tended to make the mistake of responding to September 11 as somehow evil of a different *kind* than evil that we ourselves might commit, rather than of a different *degree*, so we act as if the aggression that bin Laden directed was somehow of a different order than any act that we ourselves, meaning the United States, have committed or could commit. I don't think that's right. I don't think it's right measured by number of lives affected, and I don't think it's right in its presumed division between the sheep and the goats, as if somehow bin Laden is capable of things, and in fact tends towards things, that we ourselves couldn't do. That just seems deluded to me, and so I'm very interested in asking what happens if we take bin Laden seriously. It doesn't mean we agree with him. I don't agree with what he has done or agree with his views or his religious beliefs or his principles, but you have to take someone seriously in order to understand why they are doing the things they are doing, to have any hope of reconciliation, to have hope of anything other than additional violence.

If we take bin Laden at his word, that there can be no discussion between Americans and Muslims, and that in fact there can only be slaying and neck biting between us, how would you respond to someone who says that the whole notion of dialogue with someone who is opposed to dialogue is based on a false premise, and that we actually faced a situation like this with Hitler, whose motives were such that any dialogue with him would have postponed the inevitable?

My reaction would be different if we had continued to pursue bin Laden and attack al Qaeda, rather than shifting to an attack on a country uninvolved in 9/11. Even if we *had* done that, though, I'd still want to observe that we've made the same accusation against bin Laden that he has made against us. Bush has said over and over and over again in various ways that you can't talk with "these people." You can't talk with terrorists, there's no negotiating. If you've got the leaders of the two relevant sides, both saying the same thing, that you can't talk to the other party, somebody has to try to step in and say, we *have to* talk. It's the only alternative to the mutually destructive choice that we have made to escalate the violence.

So one option is a fight to the death, and we can escalate the violence until somebody either isn't there anymore or says uncle, or we can decide that in fact we *can* talk to the other side, and in fact we *have to* talk to the other side, and we have to whether we feel like it or not, whether we do or do not believe the other side is human and capable of something resembling rationality, capable of recognizing mutual interest. If both sides are saying the other side is not human, someone has to step in and say, you know what, yes they are. We are capable of rational discourse and we believe you are capable of it too, I don't care what the rhetoric has been. The rhetoric is literally killing us. Let's try something else.

But another thing is to recognize that those statements have been made in context. Bush turns up the volume on his rhetoric depending on who he's talking to, or turns it down, and so does bin Laden. He's also made peace overtures: look, the instant that you stop occupying the lands that we consider sacred, we stop shooting you. In any kind of a dialogue—third graders having a fist fight, or two of the most powerful people on the planet leading others into battle with thousands and thousands of lives at stake—in any kind of dialogue you can either withhold trust from the other person until the other person fulfills your preconditions for attributing trust, or you can insist on trust as a condition of conversation, and grant the trust and cling to it insistently. I can hear someone saying now, we tried to trust him but they flew planes into our buildings, and the other side then makes analogous accusations about different events, so if there's going to be dialogue instead of shooting, somebody has to say, okay I believe that you are a human being who wishes to live and wishes for those you love to have happy and robust lives, and I am going to act as if that is the case no matter what you do. It seems to me that that's a healthier approach.

M. Javad Zarif
16 February 2007

I'll open with one of the questions I sent by email. It has to do with your July statement to the Security Council, in which you contrast mutual respect and equal footing to pressure, threat, injustice, and imposition. The question is what concrete steps the U.S. could take that would count as steps toward mutual respect and equal footing, and away from pressure, threat, injustice, and imposition.

I think what is needed is a fundamental reassessment of some of the foundations of U.S. policy. Not just for Iran. And in order to say what I mean by that, I need to preface my remarks.

I'm a lawyer. Lawyers usually want to give a lot of credit to law. But in the real world, we know that law always follows politics. So political realities create law. Now if you look at international law, it's not any different. International law is the product of political reality. In the 19th and early 20th century, political realities required sovereign states to be able to wage war. So international law was formed in order to satisfy that political reality. So then war became one of the prerogatives of sovereign states. You read old law books and you see, if you want to define what a sovereign state is, you say: a state, an entity that can wage war. That was important.

But political realities in the world, and peoples' perceptions of their interest changed. And that is why from 1928 onward, the international community went through a number of incremental steps in order to align with that political reality, and that is why war, other than self defense, was outlawed. It was not an idealistic attempt to outlaw war, but it was an outgrowth of the reality that war did not serve national political interests. Now if you look at studies that have been done, you see that in recent years, except for instances such as Panama, which are basically negligible, countries who waged war did not achieve the intended results. Sometimes they won the battle, but they didn't achieve the intended results. In most cases, they even destroyed their own stand.

So this is the reality, political reality as well as legal reality.

Now it seems to me what the United States needs to do is to bring itself in line with this reality. I understand that the U.S. is an extremely powerful country. The military might of everybody else combined will not be comparable to the military might of the U.S. alone. But why is it that this huge military might is not capable of achieving results? This is a question. I'm not talking about counter-terrorism. I'm talking about even classical war. This huge military might cannot achieve the intended results. Is it not time for the U.S. to reconsider the value of this military might, and to move away from how it is commonly used? War is not a rational political option; it's certainly not a legal option.

If that reality sinks in, in Washington, then they will start looking at issues differently, and in my view, they'd be much better equipped to find solutions to problems, problems affecting U.S. national security. So, if I wanted to look at it not as an Iranian representative, but as a lawyer and political scientist, which is my training, and analyze U.S. behavior, the fault that I would find with U.S. behavior is that it has not yet adapted itself to the real world.

And, I mean, it's understandable because it's a very powerful country, and when you are very powerful, you're jealous of that power. But there are other American political scientists who have served in U.S. administrations, people like Joseph Nye, who have said that you have to go to soft power. Hard power will no longer be effective.

Now from somebody who is dealing with the U.S., you have another perspective that needs to be also taken into account. The United States must understand that however powerful it may be, others have their own concerns, their own interests, their own anxieties. If they want to submit to the pressure of the United States, because they fear the U.S., it's tantamount to asking them to commit suicide in fear of being killed one day, and people don't readily do this. The United States has found some who have been prepared to succumb to this pressure, but there are others who are not prepared. They have their own concerns. Even if you submit, the resentment that is created within the population manifests itself in acts of terrorism which we have seen in various parts of the world, and ultimately that resistance to submission will manifest itself one way or another.

Now even in Western vocabulary, to deal with others, even to understand others, is not a process of understanding another human being or another human society; it's like understanding an object. This problem has been referred to in critical studies of Orientalism. Oriental studies have dealt with the Orient, the rest of the world, basically, as objects, not as human societies with histories which are much deeper and longer than any Western society. Even in terminology, you hear the phrase 'carrot and stick' a lot. But carrot and stick is how you treat a donkey. Even, I mean, the terminology. Because what is the significance of a carrot to a human being? And a stick? You keep a carrot in front of a donkey to entice it to follow your orders, but at the same time, you keep a stick in your hand, if it didn't follow the orders.

So, a carrot and stick approach: this approach is probably used by people who are liberal minded and want to treat the rest of the world well, and would say, why don't we use the carrot and stick policy. But, that's not going to work. You've got to deal with the other side as human beings, as human societies. You've got to be prepared to sit down with them, hear their anxieties, and listen, really. We don't listen when we engage in, even when we engage in debate, we don't listen. We're more interested in presenting our position than in listening and understanding the position and the views and the concerns of the other side. So, I think what I said in the Security Council was, you want to use the carrot and stick approach, if you want to use imposition, if you want to use a take it or leave it approach, then I don't have to threaten you, but it simply, analytically speaking, doesn't work.

This reminds me of your essay "Reflections on Terrorism, Dialogue and Global Ethics," where you make a case for rejecting what you call "an outdated paradigm of global interactions that divided the world in terms of modes of loyalty into coalition members and enemies distributing rewards and punishments accordingly." And what you advocate in place of that is "a new paradigm founded on equal footing, stakeholding, and dispersion of power," and then your argument, if I've understood you correctly, is that to make that kind of paradigm shift, we need to make a change in the way that we speak to one another, a change from what in the essay you call debate to what you call dialogue, and so the question then is how that kind of change might be effected at the international level. And as a secondary question, how might individuals who don't have a voice at the international level, but are simply "normal citizens," how might normal citizens also help to advance this transition from debate to dialogue?

Well, that paper was written in the immediate aftermath of 9/11, and it was published in 2002, so that's the mindset I wrote that paper in. And, again, my reading of international relations is that we started a process of exclusion. First, as you said, we excluded individuals, and civil society organizations, and we said, international relations is the realm of states, so only states can interact. So, that was the first exclusion. Then we started excluding based on this concept of friend or foe, saying that he's with us, and the famous concept, you're either with us or against us. So that was another attempt at exclusion. Now we found, probably the hard way, that that wasn't producing results, and that is why I said a lot of developments are taking place, like globalization, communication revolution, dispersion of power, which are, in and of themselves, indicative of the fact that this process of exclusion has failed.

We cannot create a mental paradigm that doesn't have any applicability in the real world, and that is why we need to move away from that paradigm into a new paradigm where your security will not mean my insecurity. And if you read on in that article, I discuss the zero-sum mentality, because I do not believe there is any longer a zero-sum game. We do not have zero-sum games any more. We do have a negative-sum game. Because if you start playing a zero-sum game, that is if you start a game trying to reduce your opponent's security, at the end of the day you are reducing your own security, because we live in an interconnected world. So a zero-sum mentality would lead to a negative-sum outcome. We have no other alternative but to work in what in another essay I call global security networking, where you will be able to network security structures in various areas together so that they can augment each other. Not when the United States or NATO decides to place anti-missile equipment in eastern Europe; a lot of people would consider them a threat against themselves, and then they will devise new methods of countering those anti-missile systems, and then they will engage in a continuous process of diminishing each other's security, which is not going to work, particularly because we have already excluded a whole range of non-state actors from the international scene, and now they are—rightly or wrongly, and often wrongly—the terrorists, the extremists, are demanding a say in international politics. We have celebrated military might, we have glorified military might, and we have sanctified military might, that is, might makes right, and if might makes right, and you don't have it, you use abnormal means of getting it, unconventional means of getting it, and that is why you need to break this cycle and break this logic.

In that process, you need to take off this veil that is blocking your view, which in the best case scenario, is manifested in debate. It's a major improvement, but nevertheless the mentality hasn't changed. Debate is war through another means. Whereas we need to change that mentality. We need to change that approach and engage in dialogue, so that we try to create a community of understanding rather than a process of exclusion, rather than creating mental blocks, such that anybody who doesn't say exactly what you want to hear, you immediately and conveniently label them, starting with enemy and then moving to evil and whatever else can give you this artificial peace of mind, so that now you can do whatever you want to do with this guy.

Let me follow through on the idea of the zero-sum game. In another of your essays, "A Neighbor's Vision of the New Iraq," you argued for Iraqi self-determination, and gave a number of reasons for that: Iraq's own rights, the rights of the citizens of Iraq, the interests of Iraq's neighbors, the interests of the global community, and so on, but there was also a point in that essay where you talked about self-determination, specifically furthering U.S. interests, and you suggested that the U.S. tactics up to that point–the essay was written in 2003–that to that point the U.S. tactics had pursued short term interests to the detriment of the U.S.'s own long term interests. Suspending the interests of the rest of the global community, for the sake of argument, I wonder if you would follow through on this notion, and elaborate a little on that case for U.S. self-interest not being fulfilled by current practices and policies towards Iraq.

I think that the most recent Op-Ed that was in the *New York Times* explains that a bit more clearly. The U.S. always defines somebody as an enemy. Or a concept as an enemy. This is a classic American approach. There's another classic American approach that borders on conspiracy theory: domestic demonization of the enemy and external provocation of the enemy, that have gone together from the Spanish-American War to the recent episode, as the methodology that has been consistently used in order to get the U.S. into trouble. Adventurism has been based on these two concepts. That is more historical, but what I wanted to address here was that the U.S. defined the concept as an enemy because I believe some people need enemies in order to be able to govern. It's a convenient tool for governance. After defining that enemy, you start building coalitions, without looking just a few feet ahead to see what that coalition and what that blind concept of resisting the enemy at any price would bring to you.

One of those instances was again about Iran, when in 1980, the U.S., with Iraq on its side, decided that Iran was the enemy, and then everybody armed and helped Saddam Hussein to wage a war against Iran and continue the war against Iran, and then you see what happened. Same about al Qaeda and extremist Sunni movements in the Islamic world, which were created to deal with two enemies. One was the Soviet invasion of Afghanistan, and the other one was again Iran. They thought that by supporting anti-Shia Sunni extremists, they would contain the spread of the Iranian revolution outside the borders of Iran and that was a policy that was consistently pursued, not only in the middle East, but in southeast Asia, in south Asia, in the U.S. and Europe, in societies where all these religious figures who in the U.S. are now being accused of being pro al Qaeda are the people who were supported and sustained by the U.S. government and U.S. security apparatus in the 1980s and 1990s. But you see how that turned out as well.

We thought in 2003 that the U.S., by invading Iraq, was not taking into account very obvious realities. The first reality is that invasion and occupation create a self-sustained dynamic that would lead to further terrorism and would lead to greater instability. And instability, long term instability in the region, is not in the U.S. interest. But the U.S. nevertheless went and invaded Iraq. We thought that the more the U.S. insists on the use of force, on occupation, on measures of imposition and coercion, the more resentment it would create, and the more difficult it would be in the long term for it to get out of the quagmire. Now we see that that has also materialized, and the U.S. is doing more and more to get deeper and deeper into this very serious difficulty it has created for itself. Some people say that policies here are followed with two-, four-, and six-year perspectives, depending on the next election, but usually you need to be at least looking a few steps ahead of you, predicting whether there is even a possibility that your policy will serve your interests ten years down the road. And I do not believe that has been the case in the U.S.

That same piece that you referred to, the New York Times *piece just last week, or the week before, refers specifically to the administration, the U.S. administration's posture towards Iran, as an imaginary threat that's constructed to "provide some temporary domestic cover for the failure of the administration's Iraq policy."*

I had said for the failure of shock and awe and surge, but the *New York Times* didn't like that, so they changed it.

That's interesting to know. The administration has recently upped the ante with the rhetoric towards Iran, so in your view is this an isolated, anomalous event, or with the current U.S. posture towards Iraq, has the current U.S. administration basically established a series of diversionary tactics focusing first on al Qaeda, and then transferring focus to Saddam, and now apparently trying to transfer attention to Iran?

Well, that's certainly been the policy of some people in the administration. I think the added rhetoric about Iran serves a number of policy inclinations in Washington, and certainly one of them is that old tactic of internal demonization and external provocation, which unfortunately, although President Bush and others say it is not U.S. policy, can take a life of its own. And then sometimes become self-fulfilling, because it incrementally increases the tension to the point that it won't be containable. So you see elements of that in the process, but you also see a very fresh collective memory of what is happening in Iraq, which may, may—I'm not too sure, because this is not necessarily a rational or a controlled process—this collective memory may in fact intervene to prevent a conscious decision to escalate. But the automatic consequences of a policy of internal demonization and external provocation may not necessarily be bound by rational decision making processes. What is alarming, in my view, is the fact that every indication we have shows that they are producing evidence. I would be much more comfortable with addressing the situation where we have committed something bad, so that at the end of the day we can agree on what to do and what not to do.

But Iran in the real world has no interest in undermining the government in Iraq. This government in Iraq is a friend of Iran, and it's under pressure by its domestic foes as well as some of its regional foes because it's Iran's friend. I mean, look at the argument, Iran's influence is increasing, so this government is our friend, and this government's weakest point, which can lead to its demise, is security. So, why in the world would Iran weaken its own friend? Now the U.S. is in enough trouble, if, as the national intelligence estimate just two weeks ago said, the insurgency is self contained; it's domestically sustainable. It doesn't need external support. We knew that it doesn't need external support before even the U.S. invaded Iraq. I'm on the record in the Security Council saying that. So, the point is that Iran doesn't have any interest.

You see that some of the evidence is clearly forged because I said on *Charlie Rose* two nights ago that they have shown the tape on an RPG, a rocket-propelled grenade, that is an extremely interesting indication. They wanted to show that these weapons were brand new, that these are not remnants of the Iran-Iraq war, and not the weapons that we provided to Saddam's opponents, so they put dates on them. And the date that is inscribed on an RPG that is supposedly built in Iran is an American style date. It says 5-31-2006. The soldiers, or the military intelligence experts who forged this, didn't know that nobody else in the world, other than the U.S., uses this style of date writing. Nobody else. Everyone else would say 31-5-2006. I mean, if Iran wanted to use a Western calendar instead of an Iranian calendar, which we may on equipment that we build, then why in the world would we put a U.S.-style date? So, when you look at that carefully, then you get worried that if the administration is intent on this demonization and escalation and provocation to the point that it's producing evidence, forging evidence, then there may be other incentives, other motives, other objectives, that they are after, rather than helping de-escalate the situation in Iraq.

Insofar as there's an argument in these poems, it is that there's a consistent pattern in Bush's rhetoric of demonization that specifically comes out as attributing false motives to others, whoever the other is. Bin Laden is only an exaggerated example. He has made statements—maybe one agrees with him, maybe one disagrees with him—but he has made statements about his own motivations and the motivations of his group. And yet the U.S. administration—

They hate our ideas. They hate our liberty.

Exactly. The administration has projected onto people other kinds of motivations that are initially implausible. And so it seems to me that one of the points that you have made in several of your written pieces is that the kinds of motivations being attributed to Iraq are implausible motivations; they simply wouldn't serve Iranian interest.

This has been the problem. Somehow they attribute to Iran policies that not only do not exist, but if Iran wanted to pursue them, Iran would be the first to suffer from them. Now there are certain other non-tangible things that people can say and get away with, like, these people hate our liberties, hate our freedom. Who knows who hates what? But there are allegations that are being made that are not too difficult to examine. But it doesn't happen. For the U.S., you have to prove a negative, and in law, proof of a negative is impossible. How can you prove that you did not commit a robbery when the other side is not showing you any evidence of your having committed one? So, you can work till the end of days, and produce evidence after evidence that I did not commit this robbery, and then they'll tell you, how about the other shop? How about the shop in the other city? This is how the U.S. has been dealing with a number of countries, but I know more about Iran than other countries. I know that's how the U.S. has dealt with Iran.

Which connects also to the policy of preemption. I wonder about your view of the policy of preemption, given your background in law.

Preemption lost its meaning in international law after it became an extremely dangerous policy, and you don't find any serious lawyer, other than lawyers who are on the payroll of governments, advocating it. Lawyers have two functions: one function is to defend your client. The other function is to articulate law. Nobody who is not defending a state client can say with any degree of integrity that preemption is permissible under international law. Preemption was never permissible under international law after, certainly after the Second World War.

And, not, in my understanding, explicit policy of the U.S. until this administration.

It's not explicit, yeah, but you have cases like the blockade against Nicaragua and other cases where the U.S.—I mean, usually the powerful use that argument. You know, Saddam Hussein used the argument of preventive self defense when he attacked Iran and when he attacked Kuwait.

Part of what I hear as your message is that the U.S. isn't as powerful as it would like to believe itself to be, or isn't powerful in the ways that it would like to believe itself to be, that simply because it has the largest military might doesn't make it powerful in the sense of ensuring that it will fulfill its objectives.

Yeah, I think I wouldn't be saying something extraordinary. I quoted Presidential candidate George Bush in my article saying that if you're arrogant, people will resent you, and resist you, I might add, but if you're powerful but humble, people will respect you, and you'll be much more influential. It's not the issue of power; the question is how to use this power, how to approach this situation, how to deal with other people, and I think Bush probably put it better than anybody else. But that was before power.

Let me ask one final question, also referring to the New York Times *piece, where you call for "a sober recognition of the realities of the region and the inescapable dynamics of occupation." I assume you would say that a lack of such sobriety is what led to the invasion?*

A lack of that sobriety led to the policy of shock and awe. A lack of that sobriety is leading to the policy of surge. You would think that in the aftermath of 9/11 and the pouring of global support and sympathy for the U.S., which led them to take this very disastrous step, that four years would have been long enough to get sober, to get some coffee, wake up, and look at the realities, but the policy of surge shows that the same mentality prevails. And that's a shame, because the U.S. is so big and so powerful, when it gets into trouble, everybody else is in trouble. So nobody takes a lot of joy in the U.S. being in a mess in Iraq.

Asma Afsaruddin
8 March 2007

In your article on "Views of Jihad Throughout History," you point out that the meaning of the term jihad *is not singular or fixed. It has a range of meaning, different aspects of which have been emphasized at different times in history. And you also note that the meaning of the term* dar al-islam *("the abode of Islam")—a term sometimes contrasted with* dar al-harb *("the abode of war")—has changed over time. So, what's the upshot of that knowledge? How might we as citizens, and how might influential political leaders, apply that knowledge?*

OK, first of all, when I mentioned that the meaning of the term jihad is not singular, what I was trying to emphasize is that the term "jihad" itself, or the word "jihad" in its broadest application, means "effort," "striving," "struggle." So this is a word that can be used in practically any arena of life. In the political arena, it might have a specific meaning. In the personal arena, family arena, public/private spheres, this word can take on multiple inflections. When you think of the English word "effort," you cannot immediately say whether it has just one fixed application, one particular sphere. You would say, of course, "effort" is a word that spans everything. Your effort to get up in the morning and get your day started right, to go to work. All that is actually subsumed under the word "jihad" also, because it denotes all striving and struggle and effort.

To pursue the word for a second, does Arabic have roots in Sanskrit? I was trying to connect in my head whether the word "jihad" might be etymologically at some point way back in the past connected with the Greek "ergon" that gives us "ergonomic" and "work" and so on.

No. Arabic is a Semitic language, so it's not part of the Indo-European language family at all. But you would find in other languages related terms that are similarly broad. But again, if you just invoke the English term "struggle," it doesn't imply any particular static meaning. It would really depend on what sphere of life you're applying it to, because you're obviously struggling at many different levels. So, it can be as completely mundane as: struggling to earn your living. Everything that goes into it is part of jihad. Disseminating knowledge, helping someone, in whatever meager way, all that is part of "jihad." So, in that sense, jihad is very constant—that is the basic meaning. Now because I was asked to write this article particularly addressing the way it has been used in the political and the legal spheres, I was addressing certain concepts that are tied to jihad that the jurists created over time to explain the historical reality around them.

I, therefore, brought into the discussion terms like *dar al-islam*, "the abode of Islam," versus *dar al-harb*, "the abode of war." These concepts did not arise until about the 9th century of the common era, which means about the 3rd century of Islam. So they are not part of the earliest lexicon within the Islamic tradition. So they are not being derived from the Qur'an, or the sunna. (The sunna refers to the customs and the practices the prophet Muhammad, including his sayings.) So there's nothing scriptural about it, and there's nothing normative about it, but it shows how Muslim scholars and theologians and jurists have engaged the religious texts and interpreted them in a manner that made sense in their own particular historical circumstances.

The other thing I emphasize in the article, and I hope readers do pick up on that, is that very soon, around the 12th or 13th century, the jurists were conceding that this particular way of looking at the world, regarding it as kind of polar opposites, was no longer meaningful, because international relations had changed so much. Muslims and non-Muslims were entering into trade agreements. Muslims could travel to non-Muslim lands. Non-Muslims could come to Muslim lands. By no means did the historical reality actually correspond to this legal fiction that had been created. So, these terms basically became meaningless over time because you could not paint the world in such black and white terms. In answer to your question, what is the upshot of that knowledge, particularly now, and how might we as citizens apply the knowledge, well, we may use it to show that interpretations are never fixed in time.

Interpretation is a very flexible activity. The Islamic tradition, like the Christians, Jewish, and Hindu traditions, is very diverse. There have been multiple interpretations throughout time, and this is an ongoing process.

Muslims today, depending on people's orientations, often read into scripture or other religious texts what they want to see in them, you know? And therefore you have competing visions, and this has always been true of the Islamic tradition, which has been very diverse and pluralistic, as it has been of other religious traditions. And therefore when—if I may bring Mr. Osama bin Laden into this conversation—so when someone like Osama bin Laden says we subscribe to this particular perspective, that the world is divided into strictly the territory of Muslims versus the territory of non-Muslims, and they are bound to be at loggerheads with one another, if not at war, then that is simply replicating the kind of world view, for example, that Samuel Huntington subscribes to. It's interesting that the "clash of civilizations" thesis resonates only with the extremists in the Islamic world. It's not a mainstream view at all. But it is particularly alarming that that view, though, has been very influential in foreign policy circles. Huntington's thesis has been embraced by some of the most right-wing groups in this country and has to some degree influenced the way we've dealt with Muslim majority countries. It has to be challenged, it really does, because it does not represent the mainstream viewpoint either in the West or in the Islamic world. And we have the facts and the historical documentation to prove just the opposite.

So, for Americans, one inference to be drawn from this—tell me if I'm hearing correctly—one inference to be drawn is simply this fact that the Islam that is most often portrayed on the TV news is not numerically the most representative Islam, nor historically the most constant Islam. In fact, it's one very specific minority version of Islam, which—I'm now going from you and your article to a different inference—which seems to me also to be a warning not to attend so carefully to that specific branch that we create a self-fulfilling prophecy, that in essence we nurture the radical minority and starve the more open, more reciprocal majority.

I absolutely agree with that. The problem has been that the media has promoted this kind of monolithic view of Islam. Some of it is done willfully, and some of it is not. I think journalists by virtue of the nature of their trade tend to publish what is sensationalist. So, extremists fulminating from the various pulpits and shouting 'death to America!' with their fists raised sell newspapers better than saying: oh, you know what, some dialoguing groups got together yesterday, and signed a declaration of mutual harmony and peace.

You get the point. I mean, part of the reason Fox News is so appealing is because they sort of have the corner on the market on sensationalist news. And they, frankly, have been the worst perpetrators of this view that Islam is monolithic and the extremists speak for the whole tradition.

It sounds to me, also, as though another inference from this view would be its mirror image, that just as there is within Christianity, for example, as the most prominent religion within the U.S., a whole range of variations on beliefs and modulations, tenors of belief, from very moderate, global-minded, to the either-or, black-and-white approach, so there is in Islam, and it would be a mistake to think of either one as representative.

I totally agree. It would be like foregrounding the comments of Jerry Falwell and appointing him the representative for all Christians everywhere, completely obliterating the rich diversity that exists within Christianity. We have the same problem within Islam, when you, by default I guess, appoint Osama bin Laden and his ilk as typical representatives, though they absolutely don't represent the majority of Muslims. A big part of the problem is that there were and continue to be prominent Muslim leaders and rank-and-file Muslims who denounce terrorists, and have denounced what Osama bin Laden and the Taliban have done and continue to do in the name of Islam, but those denunciations did not and do not get into the mainstream media. And so you continue to hear this question: where are the Muslims who are denouncing terrorism? There are in fact legions.

If you read the Arab press, if you read alternative sources in this country, as well, you can find documentations of numerous people who have spoken up. In this country, American Muslims, European Muslims, Muslims in the Islamic heartlands. Somehow their voices have gotten drowned out because, unfortunately, the media selectively publishes accounts of the Islamic world that meet certain criteria of theirs, and therefore the normal voices are not heard. So, in some ways I can't fault the average American who really does not have very good alternative sources of information. Now of course there is NPR, we have PBS, but again that reaches out, I think, to a certain percentage of the broad American population. We have to get better at being able to retrieve reliable information, but the point is: we shouldn't have to work so hard. These sources of information should be made readily available. University campuses try to do some of that, but I don't think we're reaching the heartlands.

I recently gave a series of lectures at Amarillo College in Amarillo, Texas. Now in many ways that's more representative of middle-class Americans, who are starved for information. Some of the people who turned out for my talk had driven sixty miles to come because it was very well publicized and they are sort of tired of the CNN take on things. And, you know, these are intelligent people and they often question what they get in the mainstream media or their local paper, and they do want people who are informed, who have a firsthand acquaintance with Islam, with the Middle East, with the Arab world, with the Muslim world in general, and who can give them a perspective that is not readily available in the sources that they have access to. So there is genuine interest, and people are looking for those reliable, alternative sources of information, but often there is really no way to meet that demand adequately. So there is only so much you can do at a time. I take my hat off to the people who organized those lectures. They got a NEH grant, and one of the main stipulations of the grant was that it should really involve the community, and that public outreach should be a big part of what they're going to use the funds for. I think we need to see more of that.

One very interesting thing about your work is its attention to historical perspective. So much of our news coverage is focused on a very, very short time frame, not even extending back to what was going on in 1980 that might have significance now, much less going farther back.

It's all post-9/11 or immediately before that. Yeah. Both you and I are aware of the problems inherent in that very myopic discourse that does not take the larger historical contextualization into account. You have no way of gauging the historical continuities and discontinuities, and whether it's actually part of a sustained narrative and discourse, or whether this is something that is cropping up because it's in response to specific circumstances that did not exist before. We have to ask those questions, to be able to understand these problems better. A knowledge of history, I think, would dispel a lot of the erroneous ideas we have about one another, and I'm talking in terms of the broader cultures engaging one another.

Most people are not aware of how intertwined medieval Christian Europe was with the medieval Islamic world, and the transfer of knowledge and learning and science and technology from the Islamic world to the medieval European world, without which the Renaissance could never have happened, without which, therefore, the Enlightenment could not have happened, without which modernity could not have taken place. Unfortunately there is a tendency to write Islam out of the master narrative on European history. There is sometimes a grudging reference to how Islam preserved the learning of the ancient world and then transmitted to Europe, but then Islam just fades from the picture. That's it. It just acted as this medium of transfer and then disappeared and had no prior role either, when in fact Muslims engaged this classical tradition very actively. I mean, philosophy, the humanistic tradition, literature, all of that flourished from the 9th century on when this major translation movement began under the Abbasids in Baghdad, and then continued for several centuries. There was also a major translation activity in Toledo, in Muslim Spain, where Muslims and Jews and Christians came together, particularly in the intellectual sphere.

In a talk I'm giving tomorrow in Jackson, I dwell more on those aspects, and I talk about how we are justified in referring to this hybrid civilization that grew up in Muslim Spain as Judeo-Islamic or Judeo-Arabic, because both these elements interacted with one another in a symbiotic manner, as a consequence of which you had this enormous flourishing of the arts and culture and medicine and philosophy from which then the rest of Christian Europe benefited. So, in this basic regard for learning and intellectual activity, this kind of fusion between faith and reason, you definitely see a similar kind of world view between the Muslim and the Christian worlds.

Now if you fast forward a little, into the 19th and then the earlier part of the 20th century, the European colonization of the Islamic world was a watershed event, and led to the deterioration of relations between the two civilizational entities. Through the Enlightenment, most European intellectuals had a very positive view of Islam and Muslims. They often saw Islam as a religion of rationality, and they were of course juxtaposing it to Catholic Christianity, and Catholicism is, of course, very emphatic on miracles and the mysterious nature of God and so forth. Some of the Enlightenment thinkers—Goethe for example was a big fan of Islam—saw Islam as a corrective to that world view, that equally emphasized faith and reason, and this life and the next life. It wasn't excessively ascetic, but believed in the good life in this world. It was leading to your future reward also in the hereafter, but there was an equal emphasis on this life, as well.

Those attitudes would change dramatically during the colonial period because then the attitude became in official circles that we are the ones now bringing Enlightenment to the Islamic world. They are our inferiors; they are going to learn from us. Whereas previously the attitude was that we are actually learning a lot from the Islamic world, which had access to all these books and sources that had been lost to Europe for a long time. Once colonization became a fact, attitudes changed for the worse. Then, of course, it created resentment among Muslims who were being colonized, and this is a feeling that's shared with other Third World peoples who were colonized. This is not unique to the Islamic world. I mean, you can't blame people for being resentful of being invaded and occupied by a foreign country or foreign power. And we're still reaping the negative consequences of that period. It wasn't that long ago, you know. European colonization didn't come to an end in Algeria until the '60s. So these events are still within people's recent memory of events. It has generated an attitude of suspicion towards the West, and I think in many ways the West has not quite gotten over the mentality that the Muslim peoples, like other Third World peoples, are in fact inferior, or the Other, the counterfoil to the Western world. And from this tragic and hostile encounter is drawn the kind of the forces that feed into the "clash of civilizations" thesis.

Again, tell me if I'm hearing you correctly. It's not just that you're speculating that there might someday be conditions under which the Islamic and Western worlds might be compatible. You're pointing to the fact that they have been compatible, and there came a historical breach at which that compatibility changed.

That's right. Richard Bulliet, who teaches at Columbia, wrote a book called *The Case for Islamo-Christian Civilization*, and that's exactly the point he's making, in a very detailed manner. I'm sure if you were to sample the curricula at European universities from the 12th century on, they would resemble the curricula in Arab and Muslim, Islamic universities because they're getting their curricula and their philosophical tradition and so forth from the Islamic world, so for the longest time, Muslim intellectuals and Christian intellectuals were reading the same sources and talking about the same things. Their imagination was formed the same way. Their mindset was informed and nourished by many of the same sources. So, we're actually more justified in talking about cultural continuities between, if you want to call them, two civilizations, and in fact, the course of these two civilizations have run parallel to one another rather than at cross purposes with one another. And he makes that point brilliantly. He's a historian and he marshals his facts effortlessly because they're there to be marshaled, and you just have to know where to look for these facts.

I want to refer to one other article of yours, "Obedience to Political Authority: An Evolutionary Concept," in which you note the expansion of meaning of the phrase, uli 'l-amr. *You note that that expands from initially referring specifically to learned people and military leaders to eventually including also reference to political leaders, and you correlate that expansion of meaning with "the rise of political absolutism." You note that the expanded meaning "is replicated to a large extent in today's Islamist literature," which is "written under similarly politically fraught conditions," and then you conclude that "understanding this evolution as representing a dramatic departure from the earliest Muslim understandings of political and religious authority is vital." And so, the question is, Why is it vital? What comes to us from that important recognition?*

It's very important because the debate now underway is primarily between two groups, one that I'm calling the modernists and the reformists, and the other group is the hard line Islamists. Both claim to be the authentic voice of Islam today. And they base their authenticity on the first three generations of Muslims, in Arabic referred to as the salaf. Salaf simply means ancestors or forebears. Now the idea behind that is, if the earliest Muslims carried out a certain precept, followed a certain principle, it set certain examples, then we're justified in thinking that they, in these practices, captured the spirit of Islam in the best way because they were the closest, after all, to the prophet Muhammad. He was in their midst, and therefore they could follow not only his sayings, but his behavior and his conduct towards other people, and his interactions among people. So, one might reasonably conclude that the earliest generations tried to emulate the prophet as much as they can, and therefore when we scrutinize their behavior we're also retrieving these earliest instances of pious behavior, righteous behavior. We can then extrapolate from the kinds of things they said and the kinds of things they did to the reasoning behind it, and retrieve the spirit behind it, that is, what they were after if they did a certain thing. Is it because they understood that to be the most just resolution to a certain situation? Or is it the most merciful? What was the underlying principle behind it?

When I refer to hard-line Islamists, I use the term to refer to those who adhere to a very politicized version of Islam and literal understanding of scripture. Hard-line Islamists therefore should be distinguished from moderate Islamists, who often will adopt certain universal principles that we deem to be part and parcel of the human heritage and to represent principles that ultimately everyone should attempt to implement. Therefore moderate Islamists may also take part in democratic processes and believe in notions of full citizenship and equality for women and minorities. When they hold to such positions, they are closer to modernist and reformist Muslims who believe that universal principles of human dignity and flourishing can be derived from their religious texts and that Islamic principles are ultimately supportive of democratic, accountable governments, of gender equality, and equal citizenship for all. Because these principles are universal rather than particularistic; they're not emanating necessarily from any particular culture or tradition and therefore can be claimed by all. In these liberal understandings of the Islamic tradition, modernist Muslims will often say they are following the precedents established by the earliest Muslims and interpretively accommodating them to modernity.

But hard-line Islamists will often claim that they are the ones who are authentically capturing the spirit of the earliest times in replicating the behavior of the salaf, the first three generations of Muslims. So, they have used this phrase, uli 'l-amr, which comes from the Qur'an, and understood it primarily to mean political leaders.

And because the Qur'an says that uli 'l-amr are owed obedience, they say therefore the political leaders who are true, authentic Muslims as they define them—mainly themselves, that is—should be obeyed by the citizenry. And of course that smacks dangerously of political absolutism. So, I decided that I would go back and look at the earliest sources, look at early Qur'an commentary works, early political treatises, and so forth, and lo and behold in the earliest sources, as I suspected, uli 'l-amr is never understood in a political sense. In fact, the Qur'an simply has no term that could be used or understood in a strictly political sense. This is a reading that the Islamists today are retrojecting back into the earliest period. In the earliest sources, uli 'l-amr are simply learned people; people of reason and understanding. And they're not necessarily owed obedience because the phrase actually says: obey God and his messenger, and those with authority over you, but then if you compare this particular verse with other verses in the Qur'an, it clearly says obey God and his messenger, but not anyone else. Uli 'l-amr in reference to learned people is an amorphous term. Learned people, after all, may come from any sector of life; it's not just religiously learned people.

The earliest works refer to the uli 'l-amr generally as people of learning, of critical and rational understanding. That's a very broad description, and modernist Muslims, like Rashid Rida, for example, in Egypt understood this term to also include labor leaders and journalists, for instance, because they have their own expertise, and people can benefit from their expertise. You need not derive just a religious meaning from the phrase; you could have even a broad, secular meaning, the sort Rida is imparting to it. From my investigation, it was clear that hard-line Islamists didn't have a leg to stand on. When they understood the phrase primarily in the political sense, they referred to late works, because in the later works, this term does acquire a political connotation. Why? Because, again, certain scholars are writing in a changed milieu. Some of them were court scholars and theologians and jurists, and often they were commissioned to write these works for the rulers, and therefore, sometimes they would come up with interpretations that were pleasing to their patrons. This is human nature.

Without this kind of historical understanding, it is easy for people to fall into the trap of the hard-line Islamists, and because most Muslims today are not very conversant with their own heritage, often they can't engage their own sources.

As is true of, I think, most in any religion.

And this is very characteristic of our age. We've lost touch with our own religious intellectual tradition, and therefore what's broadly termed fundamentalism is growing. I think it finds a receptive home in such a milieu because there aren't enough people who are able to challenge them, who can point their fingers at them and say, actually, historically, your points are simply not valid. And that I can prove this to you because I can produce these sources, and I can cite from them, and look, what they're saying is completely at odds with what you're saying.

To look at the historical evidence is vital, because there are certain elements in the West who claim that Islam and democracy are not compatible, that Islam by its very nature has to be politically authoritarian. One of them is Bernard Lewis, who is at the Institute for Advanced Study at Princeton. He wrote a book recently called *What Went Wrong with Islam?* And one of the things he contends is that there is something intrinsic to Islam that prevents the rise of democratic societies. Sound historical research undermines that kind of rhetoric and ideological posturing.

What I feel like I have taken from your articles and from this conversation is the importance of that awareness of history as a touchstone, as a way of testing assertions, so that we're not beholden to any particular authority figure. We ourselves can decide with some kind of basis about assertions made by any person or group, not only fundamentalist Muslims or fundamentalist Christians, or whoever.

Right, right. And it prevents us from essentializing things, and particularly religions and other kinds of traditions. It makes us more appreciative of the fact that all these traditions are dynamic, and they're growing. They're changing. People are very afraid of talking about a changing religious tradition, but that's what it's always done throughout history. And when people feel particularly vulnerable, when they feel like they're being attacked—there is a siege mentality now in post-9/11 America, and there is a siege mentality now in post-9/11 Muslim majority countries—people react very viscerally sometimes and become very protective of their traditions, and the attitude often becomes, that you're either on our side, or you're automatically on the other side.

I would like to stand up, and I hope there are others with me, and say: it doesn't have to be this way. You know, there's a lot of gray area. There's a lot of common ground that can be retrieved by our reading of history and by the retrieval of common values. The Islamic tradition, like other traditions, actually has always believed in accountability, consultative government, that the people always have an input into how they're administered and how their lives are run by those who are in power. That's always been an essential value within the tradition. Again, I'll say go back to the sources and read them for yourself.

The Islamic world is not a monolithic one. Even though I'm using the phrase Islamic world, there's so much diversity within that. You know, one country is different from another. And there are so many different cultural regions, too. You have the Arab world, you have south Asian Muslim countries, and you have non-Arab Middle Eastern countries, like Iran and Turkey, so we're talking about different cultures as well within the large entity we call Islamic world. Without taking all these nuances, complexities, and particularities into consideration, we can't even begin to understand what we're talking about.

That sounds like a healthy ideal on which to wrap up the interview, that there is common ground to be retrieved, and that some care on our part can identify the common ground and move us toward it.

Peter Bergen
13 March 2007

Your book is about Osama bin Laden, but it's not only about Osama bin Laden, and it seems to imply that there is an awful lot that Americans don't know about Islam, about jihad, about the cultures and recent histories of the Middle East. So what are some of the things we ought to know and we ought to be thinking about that we're not?

"We" is an awfully big word—350 million people—and the fact that not a lot of people know much about the outside world is not necessarily a bad thing. One of the reasons the United States hasn't paid a lot attention to events elsewhere, I think, is because America is protected by the two oceans, so Americans didn't really need to know about much elsewhere. It's a very big place, almost its own universe. But I think, by and large, there is a much better understanding since 9/11. One of the ironic outcomes is that we do have a better understanding of Islam, the Middle East, Afghanistan, and Iraq; about places we really didn't have a clue about before. It is pretty lamentable that the Chairman of the Intelligence Committee doesn't know the difference between a Shiite and a Sunni five years after 9/11, but it's quite clear that most educated people would be able to answer that question now, which probably wouldn't have been true before 9/11.

There are some things that have been presented by the administration, that have proved to be false: for instance, that we are being attacked for our freedoms. Some Americans may have bought into that initially, but I suspect that most people are not quite so sure about it now. A lot of Americans continue to believe that Saddam Hussein was involved in 9/11 even though there is no evidence for that. Again, that is an idea that they couldn't have gotten from themselves, but it's what the administration kept implying all the time. I think there is a better understanding than before 9/11, but we should not say it is as good as it should be. I was in Alabama some years ago, and I saw a bumper sticker that said "Nuke Mecca now," and I was thinking "that would be really helpful."

A lot of Americans, I think, would say they know everything they need to know about bin Laden, and certainly the administration presented things in that way.

Their position, by the way, has changed, because they are talking to people that they haven't talked to before. I think previously they were talking only to themselves and to people who agreed with them. I am speaking very personally now, but I get the sense that they are more open to hearing different voices.

I hope many people recognize that as a step forward. I'd be very interested simply to hear your statement of why it is important that we should learn more about Osama bin Laden.

Well I think it's pretty obvious that when we were attacked on 9/11, 95 percent of Americans had no idea who was attacking us or why we were being attacked. There was a huge information deficit about Afghanistan, Pakistan, al Qaeda, and that information deficit is unfortunate, but that deficit is turning around because we have been attacked. There probably is a select group of people who have a pretty good understanding of what is going on. It is the U.S. military, because they have been going repeatedly on tours to Iraq and Afghanistan, and particularly in the officer corps there is an extremely intelligent bunch of people who have had to work this out. If you went to CentCom today and talked to the senior leadership there, you would find a very sophisticated understanding of the entire region. I have spent a lot of time in Afghanistan talking to U.S. military officials, and I can't think of anyone who didn't in the last year say to me that the problems here are all political, they're not really military. Words like "shura" and "jirga" would trip off their tongues, and I am not sure too many people in the U.S. military would have known what a shura or a jirga was until it became necessary to know it. I am somewhat positive about some of the things we are seeing. There has been a huge learning curve, but the U.S. military is a learning organization.

It sounds as though you believe that, at least within the military and maybe more broadly than that, we are getting a little bit closer to the goal you identify in the introduction to your book, that we need to understand bin Laden "neither through a fog of our own propaganda . . . nor through the mythomania of his supporters." What do you see as the results of our getting to this richer, less ideologically filtered view?

Just what the administration is doing: they *are* kind of talking to Iran, kind of talking to Syria in this new meeting. Condoleezza Rice is reengaging with the Israeli-Palestinian process, which they had just let lie fallow for six years. I think President Bush is turning and looking a bit towards his legacy, and one thing that Presidents do is they think that one really good legacy would be trying to ameliorate the Israeli-Palestinian peace problem. I think that the administration is actually taking one or two baby steps in the direction of a less ideological approach. Obviously there remains a pretty strong component of the administration that wants to attack Iran. The bleakest assessment, pre-war, of what would happen to Iraq has turned out to be the rosiest possible scenario compared to what has actually happened. My concern about an attack on Iran is that there are many unintended consequences that may flow from that. From a military perspective it would be very hard to do, because you are talking about a very massive operation, 1,500–2,000 sorties. We would be fighting a group of people who have a very large military, and it isn't a dictatorship in the same way that Saddam's regime was a dictatorship: it's more of an elective autocracy. But it is a whole different animal.

Then of course, they would unleash Hezbollah and other proxies around the Middle East at us and then really stir things up in Afghanistan and Iraq and probably get attacks on American targets around the world by the more extreme elements of the Revolutionary Guard. So, that is obviously a big concern. And then of course whoever wins the election in 2008 has got to sort out this thing in Iraq, and there are various options on the table, none of them are particularly good, but that president, whether it is a Democrat like Hillary Clinton or a Republican, they are going to be dealing with the same issues and the problems that exist.

The whole idea, the ideological idea, that overthrowing Saddam would have led to democratization in the Middle East, unfortunately turned out to be a total disaster. In fact, I do agree with the president in the long term the way to deal with this is a more democratic region. The problem is mis-governance in all the countries around the Middle East, and I think that explains the rise of the Islamic parties and also explains the rise of extreme wings of these parties which are the jihadist terrorists. If it was a more democratic Middle East it wouldn't end terrorism, because terrorism obviously happens in democracies all the time, but it would certainly take the wind out of the sails of the jihadist terrorists. It is not an accident that so many of them come out of Egypt or Saudi Arabia.

You mention the unintended consequences and unanticipated results of things, and also the sense of Bush beginning to think about his legacy. I know no one can foretell the future with complete accuracy, but I wonder how the administration—whatever administration, this one or the next one—get better at anticipating the consequences of their decisions?

Unfortunately the C.I.A. anticipated many of these consequences in a fairly widely distributed memo before the war. You know it was pretty obvious to any outside observer. To me it seemed obvious that it wasn't going to help the war on terrorism. I was sort of divided because on the al Qaeda and Iraq question and Saddam's link to al Qaeda, I'd spent years investigating it and found there was nothing there. I was very unconvinced by the attempts to link these two together, and also quite convinced that an attack on Iraq would involve the jihadists. I know enough about Saddam's WMD Program to know that he had an active program and lied about it for years, but he certainly didn't threaten the United States, though the idea of Saddam having nuclear weapons is a pretty unattractive concept. From a regional strategic point of view, that side of the argument seemed somewhat legit. So even though there were a lot of people who could say this was going to have a lot of unintended, pretty bad consequences, no one saw how bad they were, and getting rid of Saddam and his potential WMD Program seemed perhaps, on a cost/benefit analysis, worth it. And of course that view was also wrong, because it is pretty clear now that getting rid of Saddam really wasn't worth it, but in fact was a bit like overthrowing Tito and precipitating the Yugoslavian Civil War. That would have been a dumb idea; that was instead precipitated by Tito's death. But I think that it is going to be hard to think of a more counter-productive exercise.

There is an argument you can make for the Vietnam War. I have a colleague here in America who wrote a book called *Vietnam: A Necessary War*, and I think it makes a quite plausible argument about international communism, that there was a plan to take over the world, and secondly they were serious adversaries and we had to put up some markers to show that we were prepared to pay a fair amount of blood and, unfortunately, a fair amount of Vietnamese blood, to stop the plan. The domino theory in the case of the Cold War is actually true. Laos is still a communist country, Vietnam remains at least in name a communist country. So the difference with the Iraq War, the reason it is so counter-productive, is that unlike Vietnam, which did have a demonstration effect on the Kremlin, the Iraq War has had no demonstration effect on the Kremlin of this group because there really isn't one.

Secondly, the demonstration effect it's had is one of weakness, not of strength. Instead of having a democratic domino theory, as Fouad Ajami was saying, you know he wrote a piece with the wonderful title, "The Road to Jerusalem Is through Baghdad," and that turned out to be complete nonsense. What's interesting in all this is the extent to which the people who kept saying this is a brilliant idea, how can someone take them seriously any more? They were so wrong about what after all was the central question that they pretended they knew about—and the list of people is quite long. I mean a lot of them have done mea culpas, and a lot of them pretended they were not in favor of the war in the first place, but I guess there is no penalty for being wrong in academia.

In one of the passages in your book—I'm referring to page 111, thinking now about this history that you brought up in your answer just now—you seem to me to imply that the objectives of the first Gulf War could have been achieved without U.S. military activity, and that if we had done so bin Laden would have been a U.S. ally instead of a U.S. enemy.

I didn't mean to imply that. It seems to me that it required a very massive international coalition to get Saddam out of Kuwait. I don't see any other way around that. And also, we had a huge number of allies. I mean, Muslim nations participated alongside us. It was one the most effective pieces of international diplomacy we have ever engaged in, basically, assembling that coalition. So, I don't think there was a non-military way to get Saddam out of Kuwait. I think he basically thought it was his right, and he was prepared to fight for it.

So, am I also misinterpreting your sense that there were possibilities in the past to have changed bin Laden's attitude or responses?

He's been anti-American for a long time, but what really turned him was the U.S. presence in Saudi Arabia. Eventually he would have arrived at the analysis anyway, which is these hated regimes in the Middle East are being propped up by the United States, therefore we should attack the far enemy, the United States. The thing that precipitated that analysis particularly was the U.S. military presence in Saudi Arabia leading up to Operation Desert Storm. Three or four years later there would have been something else that would have ticked him off. In fact, a good piece of factual evidence for this view is that we are out of Saudi Arabia, we have almost zero presence there. It's not like bin Laden said, ok you've given us everything we wanted and now we are going to focus on other things. That didn't change their view of the United States.

So it's not that bin Laden's attacks on the United States are essentially a means for which Saudi Arabia is the end, but that the attacks on the United States are ends in themselves and ultimately United States is the enemy. Am I hearing you correctly? Or is bin Laden's ultimate aim Saudi Arabia?

Yes, that is his ultimate aim. That's what it's been about since the beginning.

Let me again quote from your book, from page 182. You observe that there is a consistency in the reasons bin Laden had given for his actions, and you say that it's "all about what America is doing in his backyard."

It's not a cultural critique of the United States, like Ayatollah Khomeini calling us "The Great Satan." Bin Laden just never addresses the cultural issues that you might expect him to be concerned about.

So why have we, now meaning by "we" American leadership, been so insistent on inventing other reasons for his actions?

That's a psychological question; I just don't know. The whole question of our relationship with Israel, our relationships with authoritarian autocracies, these are sensitive issues that we really don't want to look at. I guess it's just that simple. There may also be a degree to which the President in particular believes this. You've written this book of poetry based around his words. I think one of the best explanations of what President Bush says is that he actually believes what he says. I take those things at face value. I'm not saying they're true, but I don't think that he is necessarily lying in a conventional sense at all. He is expressing what he really believes to be true; it just happens to be not true. In fact, bin Laden has really pretty specifically addressed this in a tape from October 29, 2004. He says if it's all about freedoms why didn't I attack Sweden, which after all is the freest country by some measures. We have hundreds of thousands of words from bin Laden, and you'd be hard pressed to find anything about Hollywood or Madonna or homosexuality or feminism or drugs or alcohol, or any kind of critique of our freedoms.

Yes, that line about "Why didn't we attack Sweden" is one of the lines from bin Laden that gets quoted in these poems. Moving from psychology to policy, how would our policies change if we began to take seriously his own statements of rationale?

Well, I don't think we should take them seriously just because he has killed 3,000 Americans, and even if we did, he's irreconcilable. His laundry list of grievances against the United States is very long, and then his laundry list against other countries, either Muslim or other faiths, I mean you cannot satisfy this guy, he's just irreconcilable. What we need to be thinking about is how do we affect the swing voters in the Muslim world to get them to have a more favorable view of us? Clearly the Iraq War was very counter-productive from that point of view, but we saw in Indonesia with the tsunami relief efforts that that changed people's attitudes, and to some degree the same in Pakistan after the U.S. helped during the earthquake in Kashmir. So, these attitudes can change. It's all about what we do in the Muslim world.

Paul Woodruff

13 March 2007

An early draft of God Bless *had a passage from your book* Reverence *as an epigraph, and even though that epigraph eventually got dropped,* Reverence *seems to me to explore, philosophically, something the poems in* God Bless *also worry over. "If a religious group thinks it speaks and acts as God commands in all things," you say, "this is a failure of reverence. A group like that may turn violent and feel they are doing so in good faith. Nothing is more dangerous than that feeling" (13). Both Bush and bin Laden claim to speak and act as God commands. Both have incited violence, and both purport to have done so in good faith. But on the same page, you lament that "[w]ithout reverence, we would not even know how to learn reverence," so one question to you is, is there any hope of their learning reverence, and by implication of our learning reverence (since, after all, American citizens voted Bush back into office, leaving us collectively complicit). How might we acquire reverence?*

History is not encouraging on this score. People who have launched themselves on irreverent or hubristic paths often just continue along that dark road. But I don't think anyone is completely devoid of reverence. When I say without reverence there's no hope of acquiring reverence, I don't mean to imply that when people are behaving in very hubristic ways, there's nothing to be done about them, but what needs to be done may not be very practical. People, I think, can awaken a sense of reverence as a result of experiences that they've had, and possibly as a result of the kind of education that draws out deeply buried possibilities for virtue, so I think I could write a fantastic, by which I mean really fantasy-filled, tale in which one of these men you mentioned did gain in reverence, through discovering a hidden source of it in his own character. But I'm not optimistic that anyone would have a chance to do that with either of these people.

In your First Democracy, *you speak about education and the distribution of what you call 'citizen wisdom.' If individual citizens will find ways to awaken or more fully realize reverence in ourselves, is there some more realistic, less fantastic hope of our spreading that reverence?*

I think great victories tend to promote hubris. People who have won feel they deserved to win. Great defeats can lead to a growth in reverence. I think our sense that we had triumphed in the Cold War more than overcame what modesty we'd learned after the experience in Vietnam and Cambodia. Perhaps the reverses we've had in recent years, though not good in themselves, or at least not obviously good for our security, may nevertheless be good for our character. We often speak of bad experiences as character building. It may well be that our culture, the culture of our voters, is being changed; certainly the voting patterns have changed. Perhaps in the next few years, we'll see a growing sense of reverence expressed in our votes. Again, I'm uncertain about this because what I foresee happening is a growing sense of our own limitations, which is a part of reverence, but also a diminished sense of the humanity of the people with whom we're dealing in far places, and that means losing another part of reverence that may be harder for us to recover, as we feel alienated from the middle east by our reverses there.

Of course I don't mean to ask you to predict the future. I'm just trying, through this project, to begin to think through things in enhanced ways, so it's really the perspective that you're offering that seems to me to be enriching, rather than a prediction of the future.

I appreciate the difference between predicting the future and understanding what's humanly possible, and as for what's humanly possible, I'm very optimistic because I think every human being contains the seeds of the virtues if they haven't been totally buried or ground down by bad experiences or by some other terribly corrupting influence. That's why I believe in education. When I talked about citizen wisdom in the book on democracy, I made it clear that I didn't think citizen wisdom just happened. For citizens to be wise enough to conduct democracy well, they needed to have education, and a large part of that education, I think, is in the crucial virtues of reverence and justice.

I hope my questions to you are open-ended questions, not rhetorical questions, but in so far as I'm fishing for an answer, what you've just said is probably the answer I was fishing for, namely that we need to recognize humanity in all persons, even in those who are being portrayed as enemies, in ways that show up in our actions, including how we vote.

I think what you said is just what I believe. Learning to recognize humanity in other people with whom we're dealing is crucial. Much depends on connections we can make of an intercultural nature.

You contend that "It is reverence that moderates war in all times and cultures, irreverence that urges it on to brutality. The voices that call in the name of God for aggressive war have lost sight of human limitations. They have lost reverence, even when they serve a religious vision" (14). Is it possible for an individual citizen to manifest reverence in a way that has a public impact, that contributes to national, even international, moderation?

I think that anyone can find a way to exert some kind of moral leadership, even in a world gone rather badly awry. We forget that what's actually practical in the world in which we live in is sometimes very daunting. I think that, after all, the citizen body is just us, and if individuals can change, then the citizen body can change.

In Reverence, *you say that "Reverence requires us to maintain a modest sense of the difference between human and divine. If you wish to be reverent, never claim the awful majesty of God in support of your political views. You cannot speak on such matters with the authority of God. It is an especially vicious and harmful falsehood to say that you do—vicious because it is irreverent, harmful because it is like pouring fuel on smoldering disagreements" (17–18). My question is, how might the U.S. recuperate this virtue? How might we re-establish this difference, what you are calling a modest sense of the difference between human and divine?*

Renewing reverence is a topic I wish I had been able to deal with more. I've thought about it quite a bit since I wrote the book, because people ask that question—"How can we renew this forgotten virtue?" I give a multi-part answer. It seems to me we as individuals do it inside or outside church, in any community or even by ourselves. It's partly a matter of speaking the languages of reverence with feeling. What are the languages of reverence? Well, poetry is one of them, music is another. The language of prayer, I think, is a language of reverence. I think part of renewing reverence is paying attention, a kind of mindfulness, being open to whatever is awe-inspiring in the world around us. It may surprise us to find something inspiring that might be as simple as the survival of insects that we don't appreciate much, like cockroaches, but there is still something awe-inspiring about them. Finding occasions for awe is a way of renewing reverence. In dealing with other people, one can help renew reverence by finding the right question to ask that will spur the person you are dealing with to recover what is in himself or herself. No doubt there are many other things we can do.

I want to follow up on the distinction you make in the book, that when you talk about the modest sense of difference between human and divine, you are not advocating dismissing the divine, or preferring the human to the divine, just recognizing the distinction between them.

Yes, it is perhaps easier in our very Protestant culture to forget that difference, because there is a strong leveling tendency in Protestantism that levels the human hierarchy and also tends to try to level the difference between human and divine. Making a friend or personal helper out of Jesus is a way of diminishing the gap between the human and the divine, and I understand why Protestants want to do that. After all, it's the tradition I grew up in. But you can go much too far in diminishing that gap and it's a dangerous thing to try to do.

We've focused so far on Reverence, *but I also want to ask about* First Democracy, *where you note that our calling the U.S. a democracy does not ensure that it is one, and you contend that since World War II the U.S. "has fallen behind in the journey of the free world toward the ideals of democracy," and in fact "seems to be moving away from ideal democracy" (212, my emphasis). I hope all readers of my book will read yours and so reflect with you on the seven ideals of democracy you identify. Here I'd like to focus on one of those ideals, the rule of law, and the "devastating" moral error you identify (221), of failing to distinguish between suspension of elements of law within a conventional war (which begins and ends) and suspending elements of law in an effort to counter crime (which goes on forever). Why is "the war on terror" threatening or weakening democracy, and how might we reconceptualize matters so that we act in ways that advance democratic ideals?*

Well, terrorism doesn't have a clear home or a clear beginning or a clear end. In history there have been terrorist movements like that of anarchists that flourished for a very long time and then simply went away. The one that we're dealing with now could stay with us for a very long time. I can't see what would bring it to an end completely. One of the purposes of terrorism, of course, is to frighten us into changing who we are, and it looks as if it might succeed. If it does in fact cause us to curtail in a serious way the rule of law, the results will be very bad for us. I think one of the most important facts about character is that the various virtues depend on each other. They all, for example, depend on courage. If we're too easily frightened into actions that sacrifice our other virtues, there's not much hope for us. So we need the courage to deal with terrorism without being frightened, and part of that is learning to accommodate the permanent danger that it represents, without seriously changing who we are. We can see now politically that already there is a reaction against some of the curtailments of the rule of law. We see it in Congress, and really it's bipartisan now, which is encouraging.

Your book helped me figure out how to talk to myself about the sense that terrorism has succeeded not primarily through what "they" have done to "us" but what we have done to ourselves in response. Our own faith in the rule of law as the best mode of government seems to have been diminished by this perceived external threat.

I think that's right. It's easy to forget how important the rule of law is, especially when you have a conviction in your gut that the people you are dealing with are already known to be guilty. That's how these things go wrong.

Let me follow up on the passage in First Democracy *in which you say that "harmony does not mean uniformity. A harmonious culture cannot force everyone into agreement. . . . No government can force harmony on its people" (101). I'm trying to think through, again, the implications for me as a citizen, the implications for government policies and decisions. How do we refrain from the kind of coercion that comes about in part through a desire for harmony?*

The dark side of community-building is the pressure that communities put on people to conform. Conformity and harmony are not the same, of course. If everyone is playing the same note, that's not harmony. Harmony occurs where different notes take part in the same musical structure. Again, we just need to remind ourselves what harmony is. Let me just tell a story that is in the book on democracy. When the Athenians were considering their invasion of Sicily and the conquest of Syracuse, they thought it would be a piece of cake because Syracuse was not culturally homogenous. It had been settled by Greek colonists from a number of different Greek subcultures, so it didn't have that strong cultural harmony that a city like Sparta had. Therefore, the Athenians thought, these people will be easily divided and conquered as a result. Well, they were quite wrong. Syracuse had a moderate democracy, with various different groups in it. All felt invested in it, and they banded together to fight off the Athenians. So much for that idea! I think we need to remember that one of the enormous strengths that this country has had in comparison with other countries around the world is precisely its ability to harmonize cultural differences, which for hundreds of years has been our most remarkable feature, and one which in many parts of the world people just don't understand. They can't imagine how we can incorporate so many differences and still function, and yet we've done this very successfully for a very long time.

It seems to me that one of the stakes now is whether we can do that with a set of cultures (not presuming that Middle Eastern cultures are homogenous) that we perceive as containing threatening elements.

If you look at our history, there have been, from the very beginning, fears that the cultures that make up this country would mix without harmonizing in a perfect way. That goes way back, at least to, say, relations between the English and the Dutch and the Huguenots in the 17th and 18th centuries. And actually relations among the different kinds of Puritans who settled in the Bay area were ridden with conflict. History gives helpful perspectives. The more history we know, the better.

Juliana Spahr

15 March 2007

In your book Everybody's Autonomy, *you observe that "reading is a learned and regulated act that is usually taught in ways that walk hand in hand with assimilation" (11). Does the reading that you're talking about here extend to the reception of media, hearing and seeing broadcast news for instance?*

Yes. Of course. Since writing that, and there is some way that books feels old and like a remnant from a somewhat easier time, the media seems to be an almost textbook example of this.
The war in Afghanistan, in which the media sent in embedded journalists, seems an extreme example of this. But in the wars that follow that war, we've also seen an unusual amount of restriction and regulation around the news. A lot of it self-regulation. How news media agreed to not show images of the U.S. dead, agreed to not list the names of Iraq dead. All that kind of stuff seems even more intense than usual.

What's the impact on us, as individuals and in community, of this regulation?

General stupidity? Inability to understand complicated issues?
I keep thinking of that somewhat sensationalist 2003 study that showed that Fox News watchers were three times as likely to think Iraq had weapons of mass destruction. Humans right now get a larger amount of information than they have in the past because they have access to a wide variety of media. But they also get more misinformation.

That's part of what I was trying to come to terms with in your book, this combination of the regulation and the assimilation. As you've just suggested, on the one hand we seem to have access to more information, and yet we seem to be regulated more, and more assimilated.

Or we're more confused. But maybe this is generational. Maybe generations to come that are used to negotiating a huge amount of information from birth will be better at it.

As readers of the media—and the media broadly now, not only print media— is there some way for us to question and/or resist some of that assimilation? Are there ways for us to become better readers, more connected readers, in the terms that you use in your book?

I would certainly want to say yes, that there are ways that you can resist all these things, or ways that you can go through and do other sorts of reading. And that might be a combination of, let's call them the reading techniques of experimentalism, though that's a dorky term, to just go straight ahead trying to negotiate with information from different sources, that it would have been harder to get it from in the past. And so I wouldn't want to say that all is lost. It seems more to me like we're caught in this weird time in which how you sort through it becomes even more of an issue, and that a lot of the mainstream media sources are becoming suspect. Who can trust *The New York Times* after their perpetuating that weapons of mass destruction argument. I think before the embedded journalist and then WMD lies of the Iraq war, I would not have thought of the *Times* as the huge problem. But that was probably because I was naïve. So it is probably healthy to not be trusting the media.

Part of what I'm trying to get to in this project, that made your work so especially interesting to me in this context, is an attempt to get from the skills of reading that we try to develop as people interested in poetry, to skills of reading that have to do with current events, political policies, and so on. But I'm not sure there's a transparent relationship between those kinds of reading.

Yeah. It's probably not transparent, but it probably still exists. It would be hard for me to separate them out, the sorts of reading that various sorts of poetry require of me from the sorts of reading that I have to do to negotiate the information sprawl of the media establishment. They feel connected. But that's probably just about my learning process. I think someone else could have a different learning process. Many people have ways in which they learn to become really skilled readers and they don't read any poetry ever.

In Everybody's Autonomy, *you speak of Gertrude Stein as having a faith in "the community of the alien or foreign self," and so, again, trying to make this connection with the political kind of reading, what would be the effect or the effects if current U.S. political leadership somehow developed an altered recognition of the alien or foreign self?*

A book that's been really helpful for me for understanding things has been Judith Butler's *A Precarious Life*, and also her book about Antigone, and the one that just came out, *Giving an Account of Oneself*, but especially *A Precarious Life*. One thing she looks at in this book is the obituary. If we say that when humans die, we write them an obituary, and when the news agencies don't even mention the names of the Iraq dead or count them, we end up defining those people out of what it means to be human. As she points out, those are the divides that let you bomb other people. So an altered recognition of a certain sense of self might have a profound change on U.S. political leadership. I mean, that might be the moment where we have to stop saying things like, it's okay to let people starve in other nations.

So, some extension to others, if I'm hearing correctly, some extension of a more inclusive notion of humanity, a refusal to make us-and-them divisions that include some people within humanity and exclude others.

Right. Or a refusal of the nation state might help. Might get rid of that idea that we have a greater obligation to the people in our nation than to the people in other nations.

This may connect with a distinction that you make in Everybody's Autonomy. *The context of the distinction is that you're contrasting language writing to modernist works, and you make a distinction between the public and the global. What do you mean by that distinction, and does that distinction, made in a literary context, have any relevance to the current political discourse?*

Language writing has never felt very global to me; it's always felt very local in the sense of community-based, although it's a peculiar kind of local community, one that is more coastal than not, and one that has ties to a certain European-ness that might add a certain limited definition of internationalism to it. That seems very different from the kind of global ties of recognition that we would group under the title of globalization. The localism of language poetry has always interested me, the way that it is a kind of community-based writing that doesn't see itself as based in the community as we commonly define it, which is by identity or by place.

And I think the minute that it turns into that, it becomes, to me, a really interesting movement, in that it has a parallel with other movements that were happening at the same time around identity poetry, and it's doing a very specific work. I'm interested in how it overlaps with some of those identity poetries, even in its resistance to them.

But there are parts of language poetry that have what seem to me very interesting representations of public spaces in them. In terms of language poetry, Bruce Andrews' work jumps out when I think of literary representations of public spaces. But also work by Jeff Derksen, Joshua Clover, Mark Nowak, Brenda Coultas, etc. etc., is really interesting in how to think about public space. I guess, to me, work that is public may or may not engage the global.

Does any of this work have relevance to current political discourse? To me, it does. It helps me think about it. But I'm not sure it has a huge impact beyond the one poet at a time model.

As I was reading your book, I felt myself trying to explore the question you just described as non-standard notions of community, and so I was trying to think of ways in which we restrict our concept of community in political discourse, and whether there's an extrapolation that can be made from the kinds of communities you're talking about in this book, and notions of community that we operate with in political discourse. I'm also interested in the description you give at one point of certain writers having "a utopian desire to write social spaces where conversation, shifts of thinking's conventions, and exchanges of ideas can happen" (57). I'm thinking of my own book as attempting to create this kind of social space for conversation, exchanges, ideas, and so on. I read your book This Connection of Everyone with Lungs *as pursuing such a space. Are there strategies that we as writers or that other citizens can undertake toward realizing these kinds of social spaces for conversation and exchange of ideas?*

I think there's a lot of really great work being done around that question right now. I'm particularly interested in art, writing, "social projects," whatever you want to call it, that uses conversation or dialogue as a starting point. We did an issue of *Chain* on this a few years ago and what was interesting to me was how much work is being done right now about these issues. I'm not really sure what to make of it; I think it has something to do with the idea that the singularity of the author isn't necessarily the determining trope that makes something poetry.

That may be the question that I'm trying to ask myself with your book, this notion of a trope that defines poetry: what would constitute a poetic response to political realities?

So much poetry is taking up that question right now. Which I love. I'm wondering how much of this work has to do with the earlier part of our conversation, about the proliferation of media. In your book you have Bush and Osama bin Laden not engaging in some way, or in terms that are so separate, yet they're talking about the same situation. What do you do with that data which has become really complicated? In a way poetry makes sense for me as one of the places for that conversation to happen, because it has been for a long time the genre that is about representing complications.

You mentioned Bruce Andrews just a minute ago and also refer to him in the book, and I was particularly interested in your citing an argument that he made about Vietnam, "that a political elite uses the rhetoric of public demand that is often unreflective of actual public desires to justify its decisions" (75). In your view, would an analogous argument hold in regard to the current Iraq conflict?

Yeah, it's interesting what he's doing in that early political science work where he turns that argument that it's the college kids who were against the Vietnam war on its head, arguing that if you actually look at the studies that were done, you can see that there was a huge amount of working-class resistance to the war in various ways. I don't have the political science background to determine this but it feels to me as if that same political elite is doing the same thing.

How do we the public reassert what Andrews calls actual public desire in resistance to this sort of falsified rhetoric of public demand?

We have a lot of options with varying degrees of effectiveness. These would include not participating in the war; just refusing to show up for it. To protesting and demanding that it stop. The electoral system has been very ineffective at actually ending the war, and I imagine it will continue to be ineffective despite the slight change toward a Democratic position that we're now beginning to see. I think concentrating on electoral politics is probably one of the least effective things we can do if we really want to end the war. I feel like it's turning. I feel like that moment that Bruce was talking about with the Vietnam war is arriving. I'm from rural Ohio, a part of the country that bears a dispropor-tionate burden in terms of the number of people who are actually on the ground in Iraq. And there's been a huge number of deaths of soldiers from the area. But I feel like finally when I go home, I can hear the change happening, I can hear the kind of the anger at having to bear this disproportionate burden in some way, and that's probably the beginning of change.

Mary Habeck
18 March 2007

I'm particularly grateful for Knowing the Enemy*'s recognition that oversimplification, whether of sacred texts by Jihadis or of Islam by Americans, is a form of deception, and is ultimately harmful. But confronting complexities without oversimplifying is no easy task, so how should we deal with the imperative to listen to what the Jihadis are saying, rather than attributing made-up motives to them, when, as you note later on in the book, one of the Jihadis' tactics of war is deception?*

The way I parse this is by taking care to read captured documents, or things said by Jihadis in internal documents that they don't expect to be read by outsiders, and by looking for commonalities between what they say and what they actually do. I also look for things that they are saying not to the west, but to other Muslims. I expect them to attempt to deceive the people they believe are their enemies, but not to attempt to deceive those that they hope to win over to their side, which would not only be forbidden by Islamic law, but could be counterproductive.

In other words, our listening to them is not only listening to what they're saying to us, recognizing that the "they" and the "us" are problematic terms, but also listening to what they're saying to each other, what they're saying to other Muslims, and so on.

That's right, and looking also for ideological specifications about which they have no reason to lie. The areas where they would be most likely to lie involve things like, where are we going to attack you or how we're going to attack you, things that are very operational in nature, and I'm writing another book that addresses those issues. But in this first book, where I'm dealing with ideological justifications for what they're doing, not only is there no reason for them to lie, it's actually both counterproductive and against their own belief system.

Your book makes clear that "the center of the jihadist movement is its ideology, which must be directly confronted, challenged, and defeated" (170). If your premise is that diminishing the appeal of the ideology reduces the number of ideologues, and the premise underlying current U.S. policy is that killing the ideologues eliminates the ideology, then what makes yours the preferable premise?

I would say that actually there's a place for dealing with the ideologues as well as the ideology. I really wasn't arguing that one must replace the other as our strategy, rather that there has to be a recognition that going after the ideologues is just part of the answer, and perhaps not even the most important part. The very first thing I think I say in that section is of course we must be going after—killing, capturing, doing something to go after—these guys who want to kill us, but the second part is that that will not completely deal with the issue, and that the ideology, it seems to me, is really the center of the problem.

By dealing with the ideology, I had two separate things in mind. One is finding partners in the Middle East and in the Islamic world who have the same views as we do, and finding ways to empower them to spread a message of cooperation, of coexistence, of harmony, rather than one where we must believe that the world is involved in a clash of civilizations. These guys are arguing. That's something actually the U.S. is very involved in. Every part of government that I have spoken with recognizes this as an issue, and is working very, very hard on finding those partners both here and abroad. These are the people who obviously have to make the argument for us. There's no way that an outsider can say things like, "You're a heretic," or "Your ideas about your own religion are absolutely wrong." You just can't say that, so I think finding these partners is absolutely vital, and it's something I think the U.S. is very involved in. The second part of combating the ideology is something very different. In our ideological struggle with the Soviet Union, we definitely had a subversive struggle going on throughout the entire Cold War, and that struggle was all about getting intellectuals to make arguments, or in the Cold War, you know, it was actually okay for the government to pay people to write things that we want you to say. In newspapers or on the radio, you had USIA which was obviously putting the U.S.'s message out all over the world.

But there was another side to that ideological struggle, that was more like the one I'm thinking about as the second part with the Jihadis. The Soviet Union and communists in general were making an argument about social justice and about economic prosperity. That argument was that capitalism leads not only to social imbalance, the rich getting richer and the poor getting poorer, but it also leads to a generally worse economy for our country. They had sub-arguments about racism, nationalism, wars, and other sorts of things that were coming out of capitalism, but that was the center of the argument. Krushchev's statement that we will bury you was mostly about an economic overcoming of the upper west, and I remember reading things about F.D.R. and his struggles with this, because it certainly looked during the depression as though capitalism had hit a wall, and that socialism was the only way to provide a better economic future.

Well, economic struggle in this case meant proving that capitalism or free market system, somewhat managed, leads to more social justice and a better economic future for your citizens. So I take this for a physical ideological struggle, rather than one with words. So my argument with Jihadis is that we have to have something like that, because their ideological argument is that their system, their way of doing things, leads to a just and moral society, whereas the west's way of doing things leads to injustice and immorality. You can see that throughout the writings of bin Laden, and of many, many others, especially since 9/11. They have spent a lot of time talking about the immorality of the west and the oppressive aggression and injustices that western liberalism, secularism, and even Christianity lead to. How do we engage in an ideological struggle in that sense? Well, I really don't have an answer, but I think it's something that we have to undertake.

It sounds like part of what you're getting at with this comparison with the ideological conflict with the Soviet Union, is finding, not exactly partners who have the same views as we do, but partners who are within some acceptable range of views, such that they can live with our perspectives and we can live with theirs. Toward the end of the book you note that we can't assume their versions of democracy will be the same as our version of democracy.

Yes, that's precisely it. I'm really looking for coexistence rather than some sort of homogeneity.

Which would connect to the thesis of the book about not treating Islam as a monolithic entity but recognizing that there is major division within Islam itself.

Yes, precisely. I also see this drive towards homogeneity within the Islamic world as a whole. There is a very strong principle called ijma', which means consensus, and there is a belief within part of the community that consensus means everybody acts and looks and does things exactly the same way, and that part of it is basically congruous with Wahhabism.

Your book is careful to detail a number of specific ways in which Jihadis differ from more moderate Muslims. It looks to me as though you and Bush agree that this is an ideological conflict, but that you differ over what the crucial ideological conflict is. Bush thinks the most crucial conflict is between "our ideology of freedom" and their ideology, which gets labeled as evil. Your view is that the crucial conflict is between Jihadist ideology and more moderate Muslim ideologies. Assuming that you are correct, what could the administration learn from this in terms of policies and practices? How could we alter or replace the current heavily military strategies to make some headway on the ideological divide that you are pointing out?

This is a crucial question, and my final chapter mirrors the additional books I plan to write on this subject. I have been thinking a lot about our response, but that doesn't mean I have come to any definite conclusions on what precisely we need to be doing about this entire issue. But one thing is that the ideological struggle does include a realization that you have a discursive struggle that is going on, but you also have a practical or action-oriented struggle as well. What that means I'm not exactly certain, but it doesn't necessarily mean military action, you're absolutely right.

I also agree that I see the majority of the problem as something that is an internal dynamic within the Islamic world, and not one that is primarily about us at all. But that doesn't mean we can just stand back and let this play out, because one part of this struggle has decided that we are responsible for the problems they are facing, and that therefore the United States and also the West in general must be attacked or dealt with in some way. Now, how do you deal with that well? 9/11 occurred before we were doing anything significant in the Islamic world, so it's not as if what they really want is for us to leave Afghanistan and Iraq, and it will all go away. 9/11 occurred before we got involved in Iraq and also the 1998 bombings in Africa occurred before we were involved in Iraq, and the same in 1993. The demands that are being made by this particular group of Jihadis are things that I'm not sure we can just say 'okay, this is about an internal dynamic, and let's just keep our hands off places like Afghanistan and Iraq and it will all go back to the way it was in the 1990s and we will be happy again.'

I want to argue that both Bush and bin Laden are wrong to claim that the other side can't be talked to: it's always a mistake to cut off conversation, to say that you can't talk to these people, let's bomb them. But it sounds to me as though, both in your book and in your comments now, you are slightly altering that thesis, by saying that, even if these people can't be talked to, even if the Jihadis themselves have arrived at a point of view that excludes conversation, nevertheless there are people we can talk to who are relevant. Even when it's not the Jihadis themselves.

I agree completely. There is 99.9 percent of the Islamic world we could be talking to, and that we should be talking to. Many of these places in the Islamic world have such poor visions of their own governments first of all, and of the United States, that they have bought into often very conspiratorial visions of the world, and have cut out official means of communication as a way of under-standing what is going on around them. You know, the newspapers are going to lie to me, the television is going to lie to me, so I make up my mind based on what I hear on the street or what people are repeating around me, rather than depending on the official means of communication. How do we reach out to people who have done that? How do we make an argument? I don't think we can do it through the governments because they've been sort of cut out. How do we reach out directly to an ordinary person in Cairo, Algiers, or elsewhere in the Islamic world? And that is one of the puzzles that governments are pretty bad about. They know how to do government-to-government things, but they're not so good at reaching out to ordinary folks. I don't even know if there's any way for *any* government, I don't mean just Bush, but even the Clinton administration or whatever administration replaces Bush, to carry out this dialogue with ordinary citizens.

Maybe an analogous dialogue within the U.S. with ordinary citizens...

Yes, we've become so polarized in the last thirty years, maybe since Vietnam, especially since the Reagan years, that it's hard to get the two sides talking to each other about issues where there are profound disagreements. One of them now has become this "war on terror" and what it means, what it's really all about and how to fight it or win it, what are the tools available for us.

In your last chapter, you have a very clear strategic outline for resisting the Jihadists: "The United States and other countries must exploit the failures of the Jihadis, stop the extremists from carrying out violent attacks, minimize the appeal of their beliefs, and eventually end their war with the world" (170). But the U.S. has already started down a different path; how might we now move toward that strategy that you are suggesting?

This is really complicated, especially with the problems that we're facing in Iraq, to make this argument now. If Iraq had gone swimmingly and basically had done everything the Bush admin- istration hoped it would, then we'd be having a very different conversation right now. But because of the difficulties and problems that we've faced in Iraq, it has created difficulties for this whole ideological part of my suggestion. This is a very difficult position for a historian to find herself in. I don't usually have to deal with current events; I am usually writing about things that are over and done with. Figuring out ways to deal with a moving target has been really hard for me. I'd prefer to wait about 25 years!

That'd be great! You've just given the complaint that a politician would give: 'you guys have the luxury of sitting around after stuff is over, second-guessing everything. Hindsight is 20/20.' But your book formulates the academic's mirror response: if we would pay more attention, we'd be better able to predict outcomes. I was just reading a New York Review *article by Peter Galbraith, and his point is that* anybody *should have known Iraq wasn't going to go swimmingly, if we'd just looked at all the signals. So, I think one question is how can we take this knowledge and get better at anticipating? Nobody can predict outcomes accurately and fully, but how can our knowledge of the Jihadists help us anticipate outcomes better then we've done so far?*

The Luce Foundation is pumping a considerable amount of money into schools around the country, especially in the D.C. area, to prepare policy makers. And the big argument they're making is, we need to be training the next generation of policy makers to be more open and aware of issues of culture and especially issues of religion in the lives of other people. Americans are schizophrenic in a way: we put religion into our personal life file and then we have our public life file where we try to do things for reasons of state or reasons of national interest or because it looks like it will help me win the next election, but it has very little to do with any sort of religious faith that we might have. And the argument the Foundation is making, and that I'm making, is that because we've trained our political scientists and social scientists in general to think this way, they don't know how to understand what is happening in a large portion of the rest of the world. This should be a huge warning for us, education-wise. How are we training people to look at a situation? Are we training them in certain models of human behavior as if this is an economics class, or are we training people to get an image of humanity in its fullness that will help them make better decisions?

Two of the major mistakes the Bush administration made—and

I hate to say this because it's not just the Bush administration, it's everybody who was looking at Iraq—were, one: we didn't pay attention to religion and how it had been transformed by something called the "Faith Campaign" that Saddam carried out from 1992 onward. This was a huge campaign to basically Islamicize the Sunni population, and no one was paying attention to that and what that might do because of course religion's not important and everyone knows that Baathists are secular, and secular people and religious people don't get along with each other, so we don't need to worry about religion in the Iraq War. The second thing we didn't pay attention to was the importance of culture and how things like tribes or sectarian differences might affect people's relationships with each other. These are things we now know! But in 2003 nobody was talking about them. It wasn't just Bush, nobody was thinking about these issues.

If I were trying to identify a single passage as the thesis of your book, it would be from page 7 where you talk about the kind of explanations we give, and how we manage to impose a Western interpretation on extremists, in effect listening to ourselves rather than to them.

One reason this should affect the way the U.S. and other countries do business around the world is, we look at another country and we look for people just like us to talk to, and believe that they're the important people. Diplomats want to talk to diplomats and business people want to talk to business people, and what you do in a culture in which the mullahs play a huge role? Who in our government has the background that would make them open, willing, able to talk to mullahs? If there are no analogies in our society, and we don't have this issue of tribes and the idea of family and group orientation meaning so much more than an autonomous individual, then we don't have any place to stick that in our head when we are having conversations with people, or any way to really understand how important it is to the person you're speaking with. To many, many people in the Islamic world, it made sense to carry out an attack against the United States that would randomly kill people, rather than trying to track down and kill the people responsible for policy. This is one of those things where, again, without an understanding of the people you're talking with you don't understand where they're coming from.

After 9/11 I saw tons and tons of interviews and articles titled "Why do they hate us?," and people went around to ordinary folks in the Islamic world and said why do you hate the United States and carry out these kinds of attacks? I thought that was a terrible thing to do, because you weren't asking the right people. You're asking just ordinary folks who never even thought of getting into an airplane and killing innocent people across the ocean. But the answers that were given were very interesting and revealing. They said things like, 'Well, what do you expect when you kill so many of us? Why shouldn't you suffer as well?' Or, 'Your policies for Israel explain why this had to happen.' You saw very few people who said carrying on an attack like that was an absolute evil, full stop. They said things like, 'Well it's terrible that some people died, but . . . ,' and then there would be some semi- or pseudo-justification for what had happened.

At the time I didn't quite know how to process that, because it seemed so incredible that people would be at all supportive of what had happened. I just wrote it out. But looking back on it now from 5½ years of steady reading and thinking about this issue, and involvement in the Middle East, I can see that what was going on was this cultural imperative for collective responsibility; this idea that if one person cannot be held responsible then holding the group responsible is perfectly fine. We see that now in Iraq, with this decision to randomly kill Sunnis because someone randomly killed Shiites. That is seen as a fair and just way of dealing with a situation.

By the way I should point out that this is absolutely not a part of the Qur'an or Islam at all. This is not something Mohammed ever said, or is ever said in the hadith. But it is part of the cultures that we're now deeply involved with, and we were held collectively responsible for policies in the Middle East and for tragic events around the world. That didn't make sense to me right after 9/11 when I was reading all of these reports. Of course I don't agree with that point of view, but I think we have to understand it.

Acknowledging or understanding a point of view is not the same as agreeing with it, and it would behoove us to get better at hearing points of view that we don't like or agree with.

It's very difficult to do, and this goes back to the training about religion. When we hear things that don't fit into our own experience or our own world view, we tend to glide over them until we get to the part that makes sense to us. There is an awful lot that we missed—that I missed—about collective responsibility. I had done a lot of reading about Islam and Islamic theology in the 1990s, which is when I got interested. When I read those things, I just thought, oh I don't know where that's coming from, maybe it's just a shocked reaction or something, but now after immersing myself into Middle Eastern culture and not just Islam, I can see that that is a potential reaction that we have to take into consideration. But, there are all sorts of good parts to that as well, because when people realized in the Middle East that 3,000 people had died—it turned out that a lot of that first reaction was based on towers going down and not on people actually dying. When people realized that there had actually been 3,000 men, women, and children killed, the reaction was that those guys who carried this out could not have been real Muslims. Whoever did this, they were not Muslims. So there can be a good side to that view as well.

Anything else you feel compelled to say?

No, I'd just emphasize that I don't have any firm, hard answers. I'm still mulling over these answers in the slow way that we academics are allowed to do. One thing is that, while I do agree that the majority of this is about an internal Islamic dynamic, there is obviously something about us, too, that people like Qutb and others who followed him in particular see about our society that they hate, even without our involvement in their lands. So while I wouldn't agree with Bush that this is primarily about a hatred for our freedoms, there is something to that in the sense that Qutb, and Wahhabis who follow Qutb, have made a determination that democracy and liberalism are evils and that our desire to spread this way of life in their lands is part of our evil as well. I really recommend reading a guy named Maqdisi, who wrote a book about how democracy is the ultimate evil. It's basically an interpretation of Qutb in which he talks about issues like freedom and democracy and voting and legislature and man-made laws as the absolute antithesis of Islam, and this is part of the argument that he and others are having with Muslims, but obviously it involves us as well, because if we are absolute evil for our ideas about liberalism then at some point we have to go as well.

That's not very encouraging or upbeat!

I'm a very depressing person to have a conversation with! No, really I'm optimistic, because these guys have a fantasy ideology. Lee Harris wrote a very helpful essay back in 2002, in which he argued that, like Nazism and like Communism as conceived by Stalin et al., this Jihadism is based on a fallacious reading of reality and of human nature, and that ultimately whatever they build is going to fail. It simply cannot survive in the real world. It's fine as an ideological construct or as part of someone's imagination, but he says it's really a fantasy that cannot survive the test of reality. Ultimately I am very hopeful, because I know that whatever these guys do, like with the Taliban in Afghanistan, it cannot survive in reality.

Ross Talarico
23 March 2007

In Once Upon a Time, *you contrast "information" to "wisdom and community." You contend that we (at least contemporary American society) have allowed ourselves to be overrun by information, at the expense of wisdom and community. How did this happen?*

It's a very American concept, of course, the more the better. The truth is when there's an onslaught of information the result is immobility, but information suits the interests of Americans because it relates to our consumer culture. It's just having more. It fits right into the greed factor and the sense of abundance, which makes us feel more important or think we have more status. But, going on at the same time is the idea that you ought to take the time to process information, be reflective, be able to create perspectives from an examination of information. And of course without that the information seems meaningless. There doesn't seem to be an attempt sometimes for younger writers to fit what they've written into some larger perspective, and I think that comes from that same connection to an information age. I guess I'm simply saying that the information age has not been conducive to the perspective and reflection that should become more and more important in a world that seems to overwhelm us.

So would it be fair to infer that your sense of what we as citizens can do in relation to the situation is to attempt to give ourselves more time for reflection?

Yes, just to include in the experience of gathering information a search for some wisdom and some ideas that connect us to the community, to ask questions like "what does this information mean as far as how it affects our lives?" I just had this talk with my 13-year-old on the way to school today. She's studying *Huckleberry Finn* in English class, and I asked her whether the teacher was relating it to what young people are thinking about now, and how it relates to their world or how it doesn't relate to their world. I think you always have to ask those questions. There's a difference between just gathering information and listening, and of course listening is the one skill we never teach, and I think there may be a reason for that. We should pay attention to listening skills, because when you talk about listening skills you're talking about reflection.

Do you see this distinction between information and wisdom manifest not only at the level of individual citizens but also at the level of public political discourse and policy decisions?

Yes, I do. It seems to me that if you start asking those questions—how does information impact my own view, my own connection to things—then you certainly can much more easily go into the realm of politics and the things that affect us as a consumer culture. In my *Once Upon A Time* book, there is a chapter called Wisdom and Community, in which I state that wisdom doesn't exist unless we first of all create a sense of knowledge, and knowledge isn't created until we have an exchange between at least one person and another, and hopefully one person and a group. So I make a distinction there between information and wisdom.

I'm looking at that page: "... wisdom is not endemic to a private encounter; it is dependent upon an exchange between at least two people, a dialogue, a give and take" (64). There's another distinction that you make in Once Upon A Time, *between a story and a story substitute. If we now look at a very specific political narrative, that of the so-called 'war on terror,' I wonder whether you see that as a story or a story substitute, and how you see it affecting political discourse and policy decisions.*

I think the way the concept is given to us through television and through our culture it functions as a story substitute, because you're getting such a single-minded view of the war on terrorism. It's another one of these cases where you present an idea that no one can argue with, that no one can see any other side of. Who isn't against terrorism? If you start out on that point and never go beyond it to understand what terrorism is now and why it exists, if you don't go into the concepts behind terrorism and try to understand its origins, then it's really, it's not a story. A real story presents two sides. This is something endemic to teaching, especially teaching writing or creative writing, where you teach your students that if you want to make an argument you give credence to the opposite point of view or to another point of view. That just doesn't happen much now, so we have this kind of conservative politics—and when I say conservative I'm not talking conservative versus liberal, because I don't know how much that even exists, but just the general routine of conservative language that dominates our media, in which there is no effort to go into concepts, no relationship to the idea of knowledge. Again, it just comes across as information. And not the kind of information that you can have an argument with. I think that's a story substitute, and I think that follows the lines of the examples, even though I use a different kind of examples, in that chapter that you're referring to in that book.

In Spreading the Word *you introduce a term—deliteracy—to refer to "the gradual disintegration of society's dependence on language" (49). You go on to say that our culture "rewards those who use language to deceive others, and abandons those who use it in an attempt to enlighten" (51). So I end up wanting to draw a couple of inferences. One is that the current administration manifests deliteracy in its discourse and in its policy, and that therefore meaningful movement towards a solution to current political problems can't be made merely by replacing this administration with another—it's not a Republican/Democrat issue—but that what's needed is a broad, deep, cultural change of the sort that—to use your words now—will "provide the prerequisites for language development" (50), which are also prerequisites for citizenship in a democracy. Are those valid inferences from what you say about deliteracy?*

I think they are. Recently, someone sent me something saying that there are only two poets in America who are talking about this to any extent, and that was me and Robert Pinsky. And yeah, I think it is a problem, and the inferences you make are correct. There has to be a change in the way we approach language, and you know this is not any great insight on my part, I don't think. The sound-bite mentality that goes into the consciousness of our children from the time they turn on the television affects the whole process of education all the way up. And those of us who use our classrooms to try to go beyond that see how difficult it is for a student to get beyond it, because they've grown up on it. To use language to enlighten rather than just in some sensational way make an impression is difficult, considering what we're surrounded with. If I don't sound very hopeful about being able to change that, it's because I'm not.

Your subtitle on your book Spreading the Word *is* Poetry and the Survival of Community in America, *and I have slowly come to understand about my own project is that I am interested in trying to come to terms with the relationship between poetic discourse and civic discourse. I want there to be some more vital relationship between those two, in part because of a sense that democracy is conditioned by and dependent on robust civic discourse and the sense that our civic discourse is very—I think it's optimistic to say it's thin.*

Just yesterday on the news I saw that the presidential candidate John Edwards and his wife had a press conference, and they paid attention to him and he was on tv because of the cancer that his wife has, but it's interesting to see how the news media covers things that have that one-dimensional effect on people. Some radio announcers I heard yesterday afternoon were saying well, you know, it might help his campaign because no one's been paying attention to him. My own thoughts are no one's paying attention to him because he's talking about poverty in America, he's talking about very important fundamental things like distribution of wealth, and so of course the media's not paying attention to him because those are taboo subjects.

That goes to the idea of connecting with civic matters rather than individual, isolated matters. Going back to Edwards, he was only in the news because he was called a faggot by Ann Coulter, he was in the news because his house was too big, and because his wife has cancer, and those are things that people relate to individually. But the larger question of what we've created in American as far as class distinction and money matters and distribution of wealth and matters that have an impact on civic life, those are very successfully ignored throughout the whole media, and of course there's a reason for it. I think that's an example of how thin our civic discourse has become.

At one point in Spreading the Word *you refer to the poet's responsibility as a public servant, and this reminded me of the poet Charles Bernstein's lamentation that, "What is to be regretted is not the lack of mass audience for any particular poet, but the lack of poetic thinking as an activated potential for all people." I'm interested in your thoughts about how poets and poetry might better fulfill their public service responsibility.*

That question has been at the center of my life for twenty-some years now, so I want to give you the full answer. I did all the right things as a young poet: went to the best graduate program, studied under Donald Justice and W. D. Snodgrass, published in all the best literary journals, got a job at a university early on as a poet, writer-in-residence. However, I started making noise about things a long time ago, saying to either the right people or the wrong people, however you look at it, that we were too elitist, that we were separating ourselves from the people who really needed to be touched by us, that we're simply going to other poets and other writers, but not beyond that. And then, of course, mid-career, I quit the university and went to Rochester, N.Y., and convinced people from the city government to have a writer-in-residence, and *Spreading the Word* documents those years. A couple of pages in the middle of that book describe what a poet-in-residence might do for a community, and there's a whole list of things like visiting retirement homes and creating stories and poems for people who can't even write much, introducing poetic stories and columns with Gannett, which went to 150,000 to 200,000 people at a shot, and involving ordinary people in literary events, and showing how literature touched their own lives. It was, I think I can say, the most successful writer-in-residence program ever in this country; it went on for 8 years, touched many, many people, drew huge audiences for every program we had; got young people and old people and middle-aged people interested in telling their own story. Of course that's the basis of both of those books that you mentioned. And that's a possibility for a number of writers and poets, especially younger people coming out.

What happened with *Spreading the Word*? Even though it won the Mina Shaughnessy Prize for the outstanding book of the year for literature and writing, almost every creative writing graduate program in the country ignored it. Probably one of the most important books they could use in making sure that their students had a connection to community that went beyond simply publishing a few poems or giving a few readings and continuing on with that isolated kind of manner of poetry. So I thought that was a pretty meaningful thing, and I have been a critic of writing programs that promote the idea that we're an isolated bunch, that if people can't understand our work, it's their fault, that we're the special ones. I guess I'll be actively engaged in that battle until I die, and I can tell you that I have offended a few people along the way, but that's okay, that's my stand, and I've had more success and bigger audiences as far as literary matters than most poets. And as you can tell when you read *Spreading the Word*, there's a lot of joy in that book.

Richard Kearney
4 April 2007

In your book On Stories, *you talk about national narratives, noting the potential benefits of their role in national identity ("the tendency of a nation towards xenophobia or insularity can be resisted by its own narrative resources to imagine itself otherwise" (81)) and also the attendant risks ("Whenever a nation forgets its own narrative origins it becomes dangerous" (81)). How do George W. Bush's public statements employ the national narrative(s) of the United States?*

When somebody asks you who you are, you tell your story. You don't just produce your birth certificate or your passport, you actually say something about where you come from, and where you're going to, and where you are now. You don't just say *what* you are, you say *who* you are. In the same way a nation is not just geography and climate and demography. It is that, too, and you can know a lot by knowing statistics, but much more than that, the identity of a nation, what enables it to hang together, is a narrative. That's natural; it only becomes difficult or dangerous if people deny that is what is going on, and see it as a literal fact, or a god-given right or destiny.

Every nation has within its stories, if it owns its own narrative identity, multiple migrations and invasions and displacements, and minorities becoming majorities. Think of the United States, all the comings and goings of all those Native American peoples, nations, and tribes. There were more languages spoken in North America when the Europeans arrived here than were spoken in Europe, so that has a whole history in itself, complicated by the comings and goings of the Spanish, the English, the French, the Russians, the Dutch, the Portuguese, and so on. We need to know about that complexity. We need to know our history in order to acknowledge our story; the two are intimately linked. Indeed in many languages (e.g. *histoire* in French, *Geschichte* in German), the same term means both story and history.

It's normal and appropriate that every nation has its story. The story only becomes ideology when it goes unconscious, as Karl Mannheim the other great critics of ideology have pointed out. Ideology is dangerous when the story is dissimulated, and then dominates, when it's not acknowledged, and then exerts power over others, and indeed sometimes over the citizens of a nation, by way of saying 'this is the truth.' Not 'this is our *story,* and it's open to a democratic conflict of interpretations,' but 'this is the truth, it's a fact.' Sometimes that ideological suppression of a national narrative identity can go hand in hand with a fundamentalist religious discourse that says 'we are here because God has sent us here.' In other words, it's not open to interpretation. The danger is when some religious or political fundamentalism takes as a *fait accompli*, or a statement of fact, the story that is the basis of who we are as a nation.

Now, coming to the second part of your question, about what's happening in America today and in Bush's politics: what's happening is that Bush is a fundamentalist, both religiously and politically, and he's taking as a God-given fact the hegemony and superiority of the American nation. America is a nation that can go it alone, that doesn't need to be involved with other nations, and that is following its manifest destiny. The movement west has become the movement north, east, south, and west. I think behind that is a sense of the embattled pilgrim story, going back to the Plymouth settlement, that should be acknowledged and discussed and opened up again, but often isn't. When one thinks of that founding narrative of strangers and saints coming out in the Mayflower, those English saints and strangers were malcontents and sometimes even petty criminals, ostracized and even exiled. They were fighting amongst each other until they landed in Plymouth, and then over the years the saints and the strangers united, made common cause against the enemy, first against the Native Americans, then that morphed into other minority or threatening groups, whether it was the slaves in the slave revolt, and by extension then the black community, or whether it was the French moving down from Canada and east from the Mississippi prior to the Louisiana Purchase, or the Spanish and the Mexicans moving up from the South. There were always enemies out there, and when they were pacified, and America became America because it had, as it were, appeased the others within or at the borders, then it looked naturally outwards for new enemies.

Most nations do this in different respects. But when you're talking about the most powerful and hegemonic nation, then it has a particular responsibility. In fact, I would say in the twentieth century, once the U.S. had settled its borders and incorporated as many states as it could reasonably supervise, then its enemy became the outsider. Now the reaction was provoked, as in the case of Pearl Harbor, so the enemy became the Japanese, provoking war with all and sundry, and subsequently the Viet Cong, and then in the Cold War the Russians and the Chinese, and more recently al Qaeda and Iraq. One does have enemies, and sometimes they are a real threat: the Japanese were, and the Germans were, at least to many free European nations, if not so directly to America, and arguably the Russians and the Chinese at certain moments in their history posed a threat in certain parts of the world.

The difficulty is, do you know your enemy or do you not know your enemy? To know your enemy, I think you need to know their story and to know your own story. If you don't do that, you've got two fundamentalisms facing each other. I think one of the lessons of the Cuban missile crisis was, as Robert McNamara points out in the documentary *The Fog of War*, that Kennedy and Kruschev actually knew each other. McNamara is very interesting in describing how that war was averted because Kennedy and McNamara knew their enemy. In Vietnam, they did not know their enemy, and as McNamara tells in that documentary, when he went to Vietnam after the war, he sat down with the generals and the leaders of the enemy he had been opposed to, and they had a conversation. He said he realized during the course of this dinner that we had never understood the Vietnamese. They had told him, 'we were never for the Russians, we were terrified of the Chinese, that they would reclaim us as part of their empire, we didn't want to spread international communism but to protect our own nation, we wanted to defend *ourselves*.' McNamara said the scales fell from his eyes and he recognized that we had not *understood* our enemy.

What's going on today is in large part the Bush administration going to war on false pretexts, and not understanding the story that is sending them to war: the need for the alien, the outsider, the stranger who will constitute the nation as a single body politic, particularly after 9/11. But also not appreciating or acknowledging the complex story of the nation they are invading and occupying, Iraq. Now it's all coming out in the wash, as Iraq breaks out into civil war. But if one had understood the history and the story beforehand, this would have been different. That so few people in the military going over there even spoke the language means we weren't listening—quite literally—to the other. There was a problem of translation, an inability to exchange stories and histories. *That* leads to war, and I think Bush is incredibly culpable in this regard.

When I hear Bush on the radio this morning denouncing Nancy Pelosi's visit to Syria, he's flying in the face of what the Baker commission has recommended: that one talk to the enemies, Iran and Syria. Bush says, 'no, no, we must ostracize them, not treat them as partners in dialogue,' and that's just another example of not talking to the enemy. One doesn't have to be a Buddhist and follow the 'no enemies' principles, or a Christian passivist who turns the other cheek. We can just start with basic simple philosophy, knowing how we are made up, and how we're to avoid war, violence, and belligerence. We need to exchange our stories with one another, because our story of triumph is almost invariably going to be someone else's story of a wound, a scar, a failure. And vice versa. We need to exchange skins in order to fully appreciate that. That's hard to do with Hitler or Stalin, I'm not saying all enemies are the same, and al Qaeda are a bad lot, but that's not the point. The point is, when you go to war with another *nation*, it's important to understand the complex and layered stories of that nation, because they are *not* well-represented by the bin Ladens or the Hitlers or the Stalins of this world.

If I read your book correctly, part of your claim is that simply being able to correctly identify one's enemies is contingent on this narrative exchange, so that the current failure to exchange narrative memories has led us to mistake who the enemy is.

I would also say that, in addition to the narrative exchange of stories and histories, there is something else that we need: compassion, or empathy, or *caritas*, it goes by different names. This is common to all the wisdom traditions of the world, Hindu, Buddhist, Jewish, Christian, Islamic, etc. It's not just an epistemological exchange of narrative information or plots; it also requires that element of empathy in order to achieve justice.

But coming back to the mistaking of the enemy, I think that's a very good point, and it's interesting how very often the enemy morphs conveniently to the "supplementary enemy," as Edward Said called it, the perfect enemy, the Punch for the Judy, the Satan for the Savior. Thatcher hung onto power in ways that are very similar to the ways Bush is hanging on at the moment: cover-ups, tough talk, going to war. She declared war on Bobby Sands, refused to compromise and say yes you can wear 'political prisoner's' clothes in Long Kesh Prison in Belfast, and that exacerbated the war with the IRA for another ten years or more, and deferred final settlement in Northern Ireland for decades. Then the enemy morphed into Galtieri, and she goes to war with the Falklands and gets re-elected a second time. A nation at war is not going to throw their leader and commander-in-chief out of office. Then, having settled that affair in the Falklands, which was a storm in a teacup, the enemy morphed into Ghaddafi and Thatcher and Reagan sent the bombers to Tripoli. Today, incidentally, we see Blair and Bush welcoming Ghaddafi as an ally, and ex-IRA men like McGuinness and Adams serving as ministers in the Northern Ireland Assembly (alongside Paisley!). Yesterday's terrorist, today's hero. It's very interesting how quickly one of our greatest enemies can become one of our greatest allies in the war against terrorism. More recently and dramatically of course the enemy morphed into Saddam Hussein, then bin Laden; and if bin Laden is eventually caught, it will morph into someone else. There seems to be a recurring human need to define oneself as pure and sovereign over against a malevolent Alien or Other. Carl Schmidt and Hobbes said as much. But they were wrong to see this as inevitable. It is a common social pathology and perversion, but it is not a natural necessity. The dialectic of the 'complementary enemy' can and ultimately must be resisted and changed.

Jean-Paul Sartre says in his "Portrait of the Anti-Semite," written in 1946, that if the Jews hadn't existed, Hitler would have had to invent them. If he had eliminated them all, as he had wished, then it would have become another group. The mistaking of the enemy is almost a pathological necessity once the process starts, until somebody blows the whistle and says, 'we've got to know our enemies, and we've got to understand our scapegoats, and we've got to understand what we are doing.' Everybody accepts now the Iraq war was not about weapons of mass destruction, and that al Qaeda were not allied in any way with the Saddam Hussein regime. Everybody realises that now, but at the time an awful lot of people went along with that lie, including Congress. And one wonders, following Sartre, how people can follow that lie when they must know it's a lie. I think there's huge responsibility for not owning your stories and your history, and saying 'well, we all *thought* it was true.' Somebody was telling a lie, and it was the responsibility of those in power to expose that lie. There *must* have been people in Congress who had a keen sense of that. There were people in other nations throughout the world who were saying so, including Hans Blix, who was saying 'give us more time, let's get to the truth.' And the French and the Greeks. . . . But no, the White House and their so-called 'coalition of the willing' did not want to listen.

One of the strongest nations at the time to stand up against Bush and Blair was France and Chirac, and we all know the hate campaign that went on against France. It came out in all kinds of common ways, people pouring bottles of French wine down the drain, french fries being banned from the menu at the White House, John Kerry during the campaign being diminished because, as the phrase went, 'he looks French, speaks French, and eats French.' It was extraordinary, the venom displayed toward the French. Here you had an ally that was quickly becoming an enemy because they were saying, 'be careful: you're going into a war on the basis of a lie.' When you don't listen to even your friends about who your enemies are, then you're in trouble. It's never too late for a nation to discover the lie, expose the lie, and try to understand one's own story and the stories of others. But as long as Karl Rove rules the roost, these stories will not be told, because he's a master spinner of false stories, he's a master narrator of counterfeit plots, but he's always, like the Wizard of Oz, going to keep himself behind curtains. Still, there are the Nancy Pelosis—I use her as a figurehead for all the people who voted for an alternative to Bush—who are out there talking to the Syrians today, and maybe tomorrow the Iranians, which is what the Baker report said we should have been doing over a year ago.

Returning to this key sentence in your book, "Whenever a nation forgets its own narrative origins it becomes dangerous" (81), it sounds like one could rewrite that sentence as "whenever a nation begins to manipulate its narrative origins, to selectively apply its narrative origins, or to deny that its decisions manifest some original narrative, it becomes dangerous."

Yes, the manipulation of the narrative is what's particularly dangerous. Behind Bush there's Cheney, and behind Cheney there's Rove. Behind Blair there was Alistair Campbell. Behind Hitler there was Goebbels and Leni Riefenstahl. The people who make the movies and forge the rhetoric are responsible for this manipulation of the story. Hitler himself was a pretty imaginative, if perverse, storyteller. Remember he was a failed artist who decided he would make Germany a work of art, and we know the consequences. *Mein Kampf* is above all a narrative about us and them, the pure and the impure, the elect and the damned, the pure Aryan race heading for the Third Reich versus all these contaminated, dispensable minorities, in particular the Jews. These are stories, and for the most part the people who tell them and manipulate them know what they're doing. They make every effort to ensure that those who are listening to them do *not* know what they're doing. And that's where the double manipulation comes in. It's not just twisting the story as an act of artifice and forgery, it is then manipulating the audience into believing that the story is the true story. In other words, that it is history. The story hides as History, as *the* history.

History at its best is a conflict of interpretations. Take Ireland, where I come from: the Battle of the Boyne has divided the Protestants and the Catholics, the Unionists and the Loyalists, for hundreds of years. The battle took place between William of Orange and King James. That story is for the Protestant Irish a history of triumph, vindication, liberation, whereas for the Catholic Irish it is a story of defeat, disinheritance, and alienation. What's the truth? History *is* the very conflict of interpretations, none of which by itself is the Truth. It *was* the story of victory for one and of defeat for the other. What makes for the truth of history, if I may use that terminology, is precisely that plurality of perspectives that compose the layered complexity of history. So to understand history one must understand the complexity of an interweaving of facts and truths with stories and narratives, and have tolerance for a certain plurality of views.

Let me try connecting what you've just said with something you said earlier. We need the epistemological exchange of narratives, but also a sympathy with the other story. But part of your assertion seems to be that a manipulation of our own national narratives is essentially a failure of empathy with ourselves*: insufficient sympathy with our own national narratives.*

That's right, and if I may put it like this, with the others in ourselves. After various battles, invasions, migrations, democratic shifts, constitutions, civil wars, all of what makes up who and what we are today, it's always a responsibility to dare to be complex, to resist the simplicity of a single idea or of a single identity. There may well be excesses in multiculturalism, but it has the salutary effect of reminding people how complex and confused things are. And if you're complex and confused, you don't go to war for no reason, on the basis of a lie, because you will ask yourself, 'is this a good thing to do?' That's why Hamlet didn't go to war with Fortinbras, because he realizes it's a complex matter. Maybe his father, King Hamlet, had killed King Fortinbras, maybe not. It's what made Pope Paul VI a wise pope: he was complex, he didn't rush to decisions, and edicts, and injunctions. It's what made Jimmy Carter in my view a great President: he wasn't sure all the time, he was subtle and sophisticated. Some would say that's bad leadership, but if that's bad leadership give us more of it: we'd have fewer wars.

Look at Mandela, who says, after years of suffering in prison 'I now have power, but I'm not going to hang on to it, I'm going to cede part of it to another.' This was one of his great virtues—because he saw the complexity of things, and he saw the danger of people latching onto a single leader. We know what *una voce, una duce* led to in Italy in the Fascist period. In contrast, complexity and confusion, a conflict of different views, are pluses, not minuses, when it comes to war and understanding the others within ourselves. As Socrates says, we have to know ourselves before we can know others; although I think it happens simultaneously because it's often the encounter with the other that forces us to re-examine our own narratives. If you go back to the religious model of going to your spiritual guide or confessor, or in psychotherapy your analyst, it's the encounter with the other who asks the questions—'who are you?, why are you here?, why do you feel this pain?'—It is this encounter that enables you to reconfigure yourself in some way, by retelling your story in a different way, one that loosens up fixations and fixities that prevent you from knowing who you are and from living in a free and imaginative way.

It sounds as though that's one way of formulating a criticism of Bush's ways of narrating the U.S.: that it's full of fixations and fixities rather than self-reflective concerns.

Yes, and it goes all the way down, even to how immigrants are treated and how the poor are treated. Even to how the media are treated. When we hear the news each day—even the best news reporting, say on NPR—the figures that are available are of U.S. wounded. We rarely hear of the number of Iraqi civilians. It's very hard to get a figure on how many Iraqi dead there are since the American occupation. Why are we not getting these facts? Why do we not know the pain of the 'adversary'? I'm not talking about the insurgents or the resistance fighters, or whatever we want to call them, but *civilians*. That's not telling the full story, but only part of it, and unfortunately it's sometimes only when one is sufficiently wounded in one's own being, in other words when the enemy fights back and the body bags starting coming home, that one asks, 'are we going in the right direction?' As long as things are going smoothly, one doesn't have the same impetus to ask for all of the facts, for full disclosure. If I were a fortune teller, I would say that what Bush or Cheney or Rove need at the moment is another war, and that's most likely Syria or Iran. I think that's probably all that can save them at this stage. The 'alien' needs to be reterritorialized. But I pray wise resistance will prevail.

When the Cold War was over and Vietnam was over, there was a whole flurry of stories, mainly in the media and popular culture, about the alien. *Men in Black* and *Alien I, II, III, IV*: all these movies and books about aliens and alien abduction and alien invasion. It became quite a fad, until the 'extra-terrestrial' alien, invoked by Reagan in his meeting in Iceland with Gorbachev, resulted in political constructions such as "star wars." If the alien enemy that threatens us and makes us a nation in response to "them" isn't available on this earth, then you deterritorialize it and locate it in the extraterrestrial. But every so often there is a repressive and reactive need, especially after an event such as 9/11, to immediately reterritorialize the enemy. And if you happen to be dealing with al Qaeda, who happen to be an international terrorist group, very small at the time, you can't pin the enemy down. You've got to find the enemy, track him down: 'we will get bin Laden, dead or alive', as Bush boasted. So if you're going to play out the Wild West or Manifest Destiny scenarios, you've got to be able to locate and identify and territorialize the enemy. Hence the need to make Saddam Hussein the enemy. Ironically, it's become a fiction turned into fact, because al Qaeda has rushed into the vacuum, and probably *are* now more territorially located in Iraq than in any other country, whereas there were none of them there before, given Saddam Hussein's deep distrust of al Qaeda and bin Laden. It's become a self-fulfilling prophecy: you're going in to get al Qaeda, but they weren't there, they had no connection with the Iraqi government, but now they are there, so weren't we right all the time and how can we leave Iraq now to the whims and caprices of al Qaeda and civil war?

You contend that "in the aftermath of World Wars and Cold Wars, America has begun to rediscover hidden divisions within the national body politic and is responding by inventing new narratives of the alien 'other'" (102). But it sounds to me as though you're saying that the reaction to September 11 is not unique, but that it's a predictable, recurring pattern.

I agree, but it's not inevitable that it occur, if one does the critical work of discerning between story and history, and the therapeutic work of 'working through' pain and compassion. That's a philosophical work and a political work, and it's also a spiritual work.

To me, that's a key question. How do "we" do that work? My book is trying to understand why there was a time lag between September 11 and the collective realization of the inadequacy of our response. Bush did what he did in his first term, and then we re-elected him. How do "we" (the public, individual citizens) do the spiritual work at moments like this, when our leadership is manipulating national narratives? How do we get to more valid uses of national narratives?

Well, in part it's a challenge and the task for the media, for education and public discourse at all levels, especially university education, and of intellectuals. One could argue that intellectuals betrayed the nation by not criticizing and not investigating the structures of power and the manufacture of consent. People like Said and Chomsky, people who were prepared to stand up and say that our foreign policy is absolutely wrong: the fact that they were treated as wackos and crazy lefties was extremely sad. As is the fact that NPR is down to begging and pleading to have enough support to keep on the airwaves, to get out the only reasonable and responsible radio journalism we have in this country, half of which comes from the BBC anyway. Here is the most powerful nation in the world, with some of the best universities in the world, and some of the best publishing houses in the world, and the best technology of transmission, and it is a mess at the level of having any coherent sense of public intellectuals or public discussion about what is going on. Everyone in America should be saying, like Hans Blix, 'give me more time to reflect on this.' But reflection is not seen as a priority, and the rush to judgment is a way of covering things up and not thinking things through.

I have great hope for public discussion in America. I think NPR is wonderful, and I think some of the journalism is really super, but it doesn't get out to everybody. This seems to me to be a big cleavage in the States. They talk about red and blue states, but it's deeper than that. After 9/11 people asked, 'why do they hate us?' That was a very good question. That was a very honest response to how kids in the Middle East and elsewhere, how so many people could be anti-U.S. This is a call to examine one's conscience. Part of that hatred is of course totally unjustified—al Qaeda needs to examine its conscience and its history—but this was an occasion for America to examine its history, and to ask why we are now at the lowest point of credibility in our entire history. In the immediate aftermath there was an abandonment of responsibility, but I think with the recent elections that is changing. I am very optimistic; there are huge resources within the American nation. Look at the founding fathers, look at the Constitution, look at the literature, look at the philosophy (James, Dewey, Emerson, Pierce, Thoreau, Said, Sontag, Chomsky), look at the political theory, look at the great universities, there is so much that can be drawn upon. It's people like you doing this project, Chomsky going on NPR, Susan Sontag denouncing torture in the *New York Times*, that get people thinking and talking. There is hope.

miriam cooke
20 April 2007

In Women and the War Story, *you identify a narrative frame you call "the War Story," but which you and the women about whom you write want to contest, in part because it "cleans up" war by presenting it in neat dualities (victory/defeat, home/front, et al.). But your first way of contesting those dualities is to introduce another: that in the writings on war of the women you studied, responsibility entailed duties toward others, in contrast to men's writings, in which responsibility focused on rights (16). Why is this new duality important and revealing?*

This is the kind of objection that many people have raised to any postmodern critique that tries to challenge dominant binaries, because the alternative often seems to re-inscribe the binary. I was aware of that, but my strategy there came not so much from a desire to essentialize women biologically, as to strategically emphasize gendered differences, in other words how does education prepare men and women to behave in socially prescribed ways. Women are expected to act responsibly as nurturers, keepers of the home front, protectors of the peace, and men are expected to protect women and in order to do so they demand certain rights. So I mobilized those gender essentialisms to create the possibility for interrogating the metanarrative I kept reading about the ways wars are fought.

I was influenced by Sara Ruddick's work, especially *Maternal Thinking*. She contrasts two epistemologies: the thinking of the warrior and the thinking of the mother. But these are not essential ways of thinking: You don't have to be a mother to think maternally, or be a warrior to think in warrior terms. Maternal thinking derives from a mother's practices, her concern that her children grow up to be robust, both mental and physically, and part of the strength the mother is trying to develop in the child is the ability to deal with conflict in a non-violent way. Conflicts are part of our daily lives and so we must learn how to deal with them in ways that don't threaten our survival. It's interesting to follow her development: in the beginning she was thinking about actual mothers, then she moved from mothers who give physical birth to mothers who adopt, and then she abstracted the notion to a non-violent form of conflict resolution.

That leads to my next question, about "the War Story." You note that it is not only falsifying but also harmful, because it "lies at the heart of our inability to understand war and to construct a culture of peace" (39). How ought "we" (current U.S. leadership, the media, individual citizens) reframe the narrative of our current war in a way that is less falsifying and less harmful, that might help us "confront conflict without the automatic use of violence" (41)?

When I was writing *Women and the War Story*, I was deconstructing the War Story that emerged out of the chaos of multiple battles. The information revolution has changed everything. Anyone now with access to a computer—and the number is growing exponentially around the globe—can tell her story. This is complicating the telling of what I have called the War Story (capital W and capital S), the official version that explains but also justifies the war. Why should this one story be any more authoritative than the many others floating out there in cyberspace? The information revolution is also complicating the shaping of contestatory narratives, because these alternative versions of war are running up against each other.

This is new. During the Lebanese civil war (1975–1990) there was little disagreement that the war was chaotic, and that there was no front, no specific place where the war was being fought. The women wrote about this chaos as chaos. In the early 1990s, there was an attempt to clean things up: photographers, filmmakers, poets were all beginning to create images and stories that told of a different reality. They placed the war in the Downtown that divided east from west Beirut. For fifteen years it was a no-man's land. Unless you were a sniper, you wouldn't go there, you'd just pass through the checkpoint as quickly as possible. Everybody knew that except for a few snipers who were taking shots at each other across the space between buildings, there was nobody there.

Then in the early 90s, suddenly it became the place where the war happened. It became the front, which allowed those who had not been there, which was most of the people in Beirut, to disclaim participation in a war that could not be justified as having been a good war. So the construction of that space of war and senseless violence let the average citizen off the hook. I read women contesting that kind of cleaning up—re-imagining, re-membering— of the war, because throughout the war women writers I had been reading, were saying we're all responsible for this crazy violence, if not for causing it, still responsible each to do our best to end it. These women rejected any attempt to justify the war by putting it in a place where only combatants kill each other.

This tidying up of the mess of war into the War Story that presumes to tell the official version is no longer possible. Think of the film about 9/11 called *Loose Change*. It's a re-presentation of 9/11 through a radically different perspective: Mr. Bush and his government not only allowed 9/11 to happen, they participated in it. Step by step the film demonstrates how impossible it would have been for the terrorists to have succeeded alone This counter-narrative is trying to persuade us that the official story is false. The filmmaker then distributes the film on the internet. Now it is universally available. The more it is viewed, the more authoritative it becomes, but also, ironically, the more subject to contestation. As stories multiply and circulate on the net, we become more sensitive to their attempts to manipulate us, to their propounding of unfounded truth claims. Knowing how many stories are out there, how many competing versions of a single event, we become suspicious but also more sophisticated as we sift through the deluge of facts In a situation where anyone can authorize himself to tell his own stories, readers have to make up their own minds about which truth claims are credible. The authority of any one story doesn't "naturally" float to the surface. It cannot be imposed.

That's what we're seeing now in the war in Iraq. Our generals are trying to tell us that 'oh, yes, the surge is succeeding,' but their statement may come two minutes after the latest report that 200 people were killed in the most massive killing since the surge began.

So changes in information technology since you wrote Women and the War Story *at least potentially empower women's stories, in part by helping contesting narratives find an audience.*

Yes, exactly. In the Arab world before the 1990s it was hard for women to get their books published, and it was hard to get them distributed once they were published, but now that process is much easier. Today it's very easy to get these stories out, and to get people to take them seriously. Blogging has been hugely important. I think of the impact of Riverbend, an Iraqi woman blogger who "covered" the U.S. invasion and occupation of Iraq between August 2003 and September 2004. The compilation of that first year of her blog is called *Baghdad Burning: Girl Blog from Iraq.* She writes in a very idiomatic American English. She is very in-your-face. She has choice words for Rumsfeld, and is colorful on Bremer, who apparently wore $800 Italian leather shoes: in brackets she'll say, 'oh by the way those combat boots are just for the television.' It's important to hear how these wars are experienced on the ground. The average American may think the Iraqis have no idea what's going on, but in fact they're perfectly informed. Voices like hers must be heard. In 2002, there were two blogs in Iraq; within a year there were almost 200. It's all these young people blogging from the war front, telling it like it really is. I wonder if the war might have gone better for Mr. Bush, had there not been all this blog-level interference.

This raises another question. In Women Claim Islam, *you identify it as "the challenge" to "break through the cellophane of images with which Arabs and Americans cover each other. So as to remain open to transformation by the process of mutual engagement" (xxviii). How might "ordinary citizens" break through? It sounds like part of your answer would be that a number of ordinary Iraqi citizens* are *breaking through by means of blogging.*

Exactly. Throughout my study of Arab women's writings on war I have noticed an ability to see the humanity in the most deadly of enemies. For example, in Lebanon Hanan al-Shaykh wrote a novel called *The Story of Zahra*, in which Zahra approaches the most deadly of all the snipers parked out on the roof, and she initiates a sexual liaison with him that goes on for weeks without her learning his name. So he remains a nameless emblem of the violence of war, even as his acceptance of a relationship with a potential target shows how an ordinary citizen can take on the heart of violence and transform it. The novel, however, ends badly, because Zahra does not accept that the relationship finally remain nameless or within war. She becomes pregnant, and it is the desire to know his name and the desire for them to get married and to live happily ever after outside war that is her undoing.

I tell that long story to give some sense of how these women writers were looking for the human in the most inhuman. The sniper is human; teenagers with their Kalishnakovs are humans with whom one should be able to speak, like our children they should be able to listen to reason and because they are humans one should be able to prevent them from committing atrocities. In international war blogs we can read this call for attention to the human. I find hope from writings of these young "netizens," citizens of the net.

That may be an example of what in Women Claim Islam *you call "strategic self-positioning" (59). Am I right to read in your book a "two-level" argument, not only that Muslim women are in fact practicing strategic self-positioning, but also that we (persons who are not Muslim women) ought to follow their example of adopting strategic self-positionings rather than asserting a (purportedly) coherent identity?*

Absolutely. Even if unconsciously, we are constantly repositioning ourselves. We say different things to different people depending on which aspect of our perceived identity we want to highlight, particularly if we feel threatened. It does not matter that I'm an American until I'm in some situation where to be American is relevant. This is true for me as a white, middle class professor of Arab culture in this post 9/11 world. We position and reposition ourselves vis-à-vis interlocutors. Since 9/11 Muslim women have become very prominent. They represent their community's norms and values and as such they are finding it harder and harder to function beyond the coherent, homogeneous label that I call Muslimwoman (one word). Some are saying 'ok, fine, you think I'm a Muslim woman, so I'll act in terms of what you say I am, but I'll use that label to empower myself.'

I may be taking things too far now, but I'm thinking of the relationship between the two books, and wondering whether asserting a coherent identity relates to focusing on rights, and strategic self-positioning relates to responsibility toward others, the more feminine approach to narrative from your earlier book. The assertion of coherent identity seems to be a kind of putting oneself forward as when one asserts one's rights; responsibilities seem more reciprocal.

Yes, the projection of a coherent Muslimwoman identity does allow for the articulation of a rights language. That's why I named the book *Women Claim Islam*, because it is by drawing attention to the ways in which they discharge their religious responsibilities that women can claim their rights in Islam. Some women have been exploiting the Muslimwoman label. Consider Ayaan Hirsi Ali, a Somali woman who has just published a book called *The Infidel*. In 2004 she made a film with a Dutch filmmaker named Theo van Gogh. He was the Don Imus of Holland, and the two of them collaborated to make a film called *Submission*. Quranic verses are projected on to the naked, whipped bodies of veiled women, to show how awful Islam is to women. Theo van Gogh was stabbed to death by a Moroccan who left on the knife a letter to explain why he was being killed and threatening Ayaan Hirsi Ali. She then fled Holland and was welcomed with open arms by the American Enterprise Institute. She is now touring around the country giving talks about the film and her book *The Infidel* that allow for no audience Q&A, just a super-slick presentation about how I as a Muslim woman can tell you about the brutality of Islam. So that's the negative side to the new prominence of Muslim women.

Am I right to hear you saying that one problem with this no-question-and-answer presentation is how singular it is? It presents a single point of view, and admits of no contestation of that point of view, but in Women Claim Islam *you advocate what you call a "fluid discursive strategy" of "multiple critique," without which many people are silenced by the master narrative. How do we get those who have been empowered by master narratives (e.g.*

George W. Bush) to learn the strategy of multiple critique, rather than simply speaking from the master narrative?

I think George Bush would be completely disinterested in learning any discursive style other than his own, because he has absolute power, at least for the time being. For him the world is black and white, good and evil, true and false, and that is the problem. It's also part of the problem that I have had in conversation with military historians who have expressed interest in gendered approaches to the study of war. Once in the conversation they generally decide 'This is way too complicated. We can't think about gender during war, when we have to deal with life and death issues.' I am less concerned with strategies and tactics, with peace talks and immediate resolutions, than I am with how history is going to read us. What will history make of the fact that people around the world, people from so-called enemy nations, not only can live together but want to live together and their leaders will not let this happen?

Just this morning there was a powerful example of this on NPR. It was a story about a Sudanese woman in Israel. This Sudanese woman escaped with her children from Dharfur to Egypt where she ended up in a refugee community. She was abused and one of her daughters was raped, and she said, 'well, there's no way I'm going to stay here because I can't protect my children,' so she decided she would simply walk away. She walked and walked and walked. Eventually she arrived at the Israeli border, where she was taken in by a couple of Israeli soldiers. She was taken to a women's shelter where she stayed for a few months. Now government officials have become aware of her, and they're saying that this Sudanese woman who's been taken in by Israeli women comes from a country with which Israel is at war and so she needs to leave Israel because she might be an enemy agent.'

It's hard for me to deal with the fact that I'm becoming pessimistic. I have always been an inveterate optimist. But the situation in the Middle East is *so* much worse than it has ever been before. I know Israelis and I know Palestinians, and I know that they often like each other, recognize each other in a way that is uncanny, sometimes fall in love with each other, try to live together, and establish peace communities. But then at that moment when all seems to be going in the right direction, some official will come and destroy that relationship. One of the most moving examples is that of Mahmoud Darwish, Palestine's best-known poet, who was six or seven when the Israeli state was established. As a young man he had an affair with a Jewish girl, Rita, and he wrote poems to her. Then one day she comes back after having been gone for a while and she is wearing an army uniform—Israelis, you know, have compulsory military service. The uniform made their love impossible. Just as the Israeli state is now intervening between the Sudanese woman and her Israeli women friends and protectors, so the uniform intervened between Rita and Mahmoud. And how many experiments in living together have idealistic Palestinians and Israelis conducted over the years? I've seen this so often that I can hardly bear to think about the peace process or anything, I feel like sticking my head in the sand.

If I were encapsulating what I hear from this conversation and from your books, though, it isn't finally about optimism or pessimism. It's an imperative, an imploring really: whether or not we can influence the large-scale events, whether or not we can keep uniforms from intervening, we still have a responsibility to keep telling alternative stories.

Yes. Even when it feels lonely and pointless.

Pheng Cheah
1 May 2007

Your book Inhuman Conditions *locates human rights within the field of globalization, rather than as a transcendental check on the effects of globalization. The current U.S. administration regularly appeals to the transcendental (good vs. evil, etc.) as a rationale for its attempts to manage the distribution of rights: e.g. its purported according of rights to the citizens of Afghanistan and Iraq, and the actual denial of rights to persons detained in Guantánamo. How might policy be framed differently if U.S. leadership held a view of the origin and nature of human rights that was, according to your book, more sound?*

We generally say that human rights are innate or natural, and therefore that they're history-transcendent. But they are only activated, asserted, or claimed within concrete historical contexts, so it seems to me that human rights are the best examples of performatives. We say that people are born with human rights, but in fact we have to be taught that we have them and that we can claim them. You see this performative positing of a right at work in the situations that you describe in your question. The U.S. claims that it is asserting or making effective these rights for the citizens of Afghanistan and Iraq, but it is only able to assert these rights by virtue of its geopolitical position as the only remaining superpower in the world today. So these rights are inseparable from the benevolence of the U.S. On the other hand, the detainees at Guantánamo should have every human right that the U.S. is claiming on behalf of the citizens of Afghanistan and Iraq, but the U.S. is here deciding that it's trumping these rights and suspending them in the interest of national security, and by invoking a situation of emergency, implicitly revealing that rights are not really as unconditional as they're claimed to be. They always arise, or they're activated, under quite concrete conditions, and they arise from various negotiations.

Once you acknowledge this observation about human rights, both the U.S. citizenry and the state have to give up the arrogance of tone when they claim to be the champion of human rights. The U.S., both the people and the state, have to acknowledge that they are in a position to make this claim (that other people have their rights violated, and the U.S. is able to champion the rights of other people) because of U.S. economic and military superiority. And I think it's the case that some of the specific human rights that they claim are being violated elsewhere *are* being violated, and they should be asserted. But it is one thing for these rights to be claimed by the Iraqi or Afghani people, in terms of their own struggle against the state that is violating those rights, and another for the U.S. to claim it for them. If the U.S. claims it for them, then since self-determination, the self-determination of a people, is in fact also a human right, the U.S. claim of asserting rights for other people is also a violation of the human right of self-determination of those people. That's another indication of how human rights are never unconditional, but always negotiations, because here you have human rights that clash with each other.

The U.S. should also acknowledge that some of these human rights violations are occurring because the U.S. itself is complicit with, and probably the major player in, the kind of economic exploitation that is brought about by capitalist globalization. Let me give you another example, which is not from this very obvious crisis of the war in Iraq. The Bush campaign against the trafficking of women for the purposes of sexual exploitation is always about saving women from other cultures. The Bush government condemns what it says are barbaric practices of other cultures, usually Asian. But what is left out of the picture is that the material conditions that lead to this kind of sexual trafficking are actually created by neo-liberal globalization, and the U.S. is a major player in this theater.

So for instance in the case of Thailand, for women from impoverished rural areas that are left aside by the influx of foreign capital, prostitution is often the only way for them to help their families survive economically. The World Bank is promoting tourism as a source of foreign exchange, and as a means to rapid economic development, but what is ignored is that sexual tourism is often an unacknowledged part of tourism. So the whole global economic structure is such that countries are often implicitly told they have to pimp their young women and girls, either as cheap labor for foreign factories, or as migrant domestic workers to be exploited overseas, or as sex workers to be trafficked elsewhere. All of this is tacit. The human rights violations of young women who are sex workers occur partly because at the level of economic development this is what the policies of international bodies dictate to developing countries.

If I were told that you or anyone was arguing that human rights are not absolute, but are performative and culturally conditioned, I would initially think of this as a weakening of human rights and of the responsibilities of powerful nations toward human rights, but what I'm hearing from you is that there's an increased *obligation to human rights, both in terms of avoiding complicity, through the economic structure, and maintaining consistency, so that if we demand certain rights for our own citizens, we also accord those rights to others.*

Yes. If any affirmation of human rights or any claim to human rights is contaminated, it's not that you throw up your hands and say 'then let's just throw everything away and lapse into cynicism and nihilism.' Instead, you have to become more and more vigilant, and more and more responsible. Because at bottom the question is why people feel that certain things that we call human rights are being violated. Something there calls for responsibility. But when we respond—responsibility is a matter of responding— when we respond to something, we calculate, we rationalize, and so forth. We say our responsibility stops here because our reason has taken enough account, but I'm saying here that, no, you cannot ever take enough account; it's a matter of accounting interminably, because we are always imbricated in a set of conditions that engender exploitation. So there is the unconditional, on the one hand, which is to say whatever it is that prompts us to respond, but then we can only respond under certain conditions. So we traffic with the unconditional, and the responsibility has to be inter-minable because it comes from outside us and exceeds us.

That notion of interminability seems important. You suggest that we ought "to reconceptualize freedom in terms of an interminable negotiation with and responsibility to the forces that give us ourselves instead of the transcendence of the given" (79). In the discourse of U.S. politics, freedom is treated as a given, something we possess once for all and distribute to others, as in Afghanistan and Iraq. What would be the tangible effects if U.S. policymakers—including in that group voting citizens—recognized freedom as the effect of an interminable negotiation?

Just to continue with this train of thought, much of what I just said about human rights applies also to freedom. Just as human rights need to be activated, so too, freedom, as Marx taught us, is not an abstract power but a concrete capacity, and is, therefore, inseparable from material conditions that enable freedom to be attained or exercised. So if you say a U.S. citizen possesses freedom, it's not because the U.S. citizen is wiser, or better educated, and therefore conscious that human beings are free. They may be better educated, or they may be indoctrinated in the rhetoric that they are free, but this is because of the existence of a material infrastructure that includes compulsory education, and this is possible because of the powerful place of the U.S. in the global economic order. The economic power of the U.S., I want to suggest, is achieved at the expense of other countries, because capitalism is an unequal and competitive system of accumulation, and many other countries are not able to provide the welfare services and conditions for social development, because poverty compels them to institute exploitative working conditions for their citizens so they can attract transnational capital investment. So the first tangible effect of recognizing that freedom is the product of interminable negotiation, is acknowledging that U.S. people are free at the expense of other people who are deprived of freedom, and this is the condition of the possibility of freedom in the U.S.

Second, true freedom would then have to be achieved at a global level. The bottom line is economic redistribution, forgiveness of debt, the redressing of centuries of colonialism and also contemporary neo-colonialism with regard to Africa, and neo-liberal globalization with regard to Asia and Latin America. The other thing to be addressed would be the international division of labor and the creation and maintenance of a hierarchy of knowledge-rich and knowledge-poor countries through the TRIPS agreement.

Third, it is, after all, unclear that U.S. citizens are free according to the most generous sense of the term. For instance, there is no national health care system in the country. Social welfare here is very limited in comparison to many European states. All of this would have to be taken into account when you recognize that freedom comes from interminable negotiation. It's not something that you possess once and for all. It's not something that you can go and give to other people. So reconceptualizing freedom in terms of an interminable negotiation would lead to trying to investigate the conditions that make you free in comparison to other people.

I'm hearing you question the premise that what makes me free can, in principle, make everyone else free. Also I'm hearing you question whether the dominant use in the U.S. of the word freedom actually names true freedom.

The dominant use of the word freedom refers to the freedom of the individual. The same with human rights. When the Bush administration talks about human rights, they have in mind civil and political liberties of the individual. So, for instance, freedoms such as economic freedom are not part of the Bush administration's account of freedom. If you take this liberal individualist idea of freedom as the only definition of freedom, then the freedom that you have in mind is really an abstract principle, and if you can have freedom in this sense, other people can have it simply because we are all human. There's no understanding of freedom as something that is asserted in a collective or a global setting. Whereas if you understand freedom as something that can only be achieved in a global setting, you have to acknowledge that what makes you free does not necessarily make other people free. It could be quite the opposite, that what enables you to be free takes freedom away from other people.

You can claim to be free, but the condition or possibility of your freedom is in fact the exploitation of other people. To say this freedom that I have is exportable, so to speak, is already to assume a logic of commodification that treats freedom like a packaged product that you can export elsewhere. And once again there's a whole structure of unequal exchange, distribution, exploitation, and so on, that all comes into play, but is not acknowledged. To be aware of the relational character of freedom, as opposed to an atomistic view of freedom, would then require us to think about freedom globally, which would then lead to a certain kind of interminable vigilance, because freedom is not yet attained at that global level.

So freedom would have to be construed as related to distributive justice, not only as an atomized thing that one person or one nation independently might obtain, but as a part of or an effect of . . .

. . . broader structures of distribution, yes. Think once again of this idea of my freedom as something I possess, something that is my property. Of course property or possession is used metaphorically. But that still presupposes freedom as an effect of a network of exchange and distribution, because there is no private property without exchange and distribution. So the very way that freedom is conventionally conceived already presupposes a system of exploitation. If one is to be vigilant about that, the whole question of redistribution would have to enter into the picture. So your point that the collective notion of freedom or a relational notion of freedom necessarily implies a notion of distributive justice, I think, is a very good way of putting it. But distribution is not something that can occur once and for all. Everything will have to be repeatedly calibrated, so to speak.

In contrast to your view that "all visions of specific human rights are open to contestation" (156), U.S. policymakers claim the prerogative to contest the visions of human rights held by other nations, but regard "our" vision of human rights as immune from contestation. Is there hope that this situation might change, and what would be the results of such a change?

My point was that the right to rights, which issues from what is called human dignity, is without content, and because it's without content, it is contestable in terms of which specific rights need to be elaborated. So if you look at the history of human rights—and one forgets that human rights have a history—there are various regimes of human rights: first-generation human rights, second-generation human rights, and third-generation human rights. The first generation of human rights are the civil and political liberties of the individual, those linked to the French Revolution, the bourgeois revolution. The second generation of rights are the social and economic rights linked to the socialist revolution. The third generation consists of the right to development, which is tied to the struggles for decolonization after the second world war. Historically, human rights are constantly being contested, and this historicity, this impulse toward perfectibility, is already built into the idea of human rights because the right to rights is contentless.

You're right to point out that U.S. policymakers think of their own vision of rights as immune to contestation, so that in general the operations of Human Rights Watch are largely directed at countries outside the North Atlantic, as though they are the only people who violate human rights. The citizens and states of the North Atlantic are the upholders of rights, the champions of humanity. I think a change would be beneficial, that U.S. policymakers need also to acknowledge that their vision of human rights is not immune to contestation, but I think it's unlikely that that change will happen. If it were to happen, it would need to be followed by genuine dialogue, where human rights are repeatedly negotiated, and not just between states. Some of this dialogue is happening at the World Social Forum. But states need to be open and receptive. And NGOs are not always pure since they are funded from different sources and represent different interests. For change to happen, it cannot be just a top-down change at the level of U.S. policymakers; there needs to be some movement from the bottom, but this movement also needs to be received by people at the top.

In the interviews for this book, it certainly has been a theme, this need for dialogue.

Dialogue is a complicated term and a complicated phenomenon, because if the dialogue is global then it will always occur between different cultures and different languages. Therefore there will always be translation, and with translation there is always violence done to the singularity of the other. So dialogue itself is a negotiation, not a transparent communication.

The last paragraph of your book speaks of "the small contaminated victories of human rights" (265). How might those of us who feel both small and contaminated ourselves (as citizens of a U.S. whose recent deformations of human rights have been flagrant) achieve such victories?

What I'm going to say sounds like a cliché, but here it is. You can only begin where you are. If you're a taxpayer and a voter in the U.S., then you're in a much better position than many other people elsewhere. The other thing that you and I share is that we are both teachers at institutions of higher learning. So one immediate thing to do is to try to make students aware of situations in which the U.S. is deeply complicit with the human rights violations that it openly denounces. Students are the future voters, and I think there's no way around it: electoral education is crucial.

With my own students, I use the example of Ikea. If you go to Ikea, you can buy eight wooden coathangers for $2.99, and you can do that because the wood is obtained very cheaply in China, since they have many forests they can cut down. The hangers are manufactured by workers who are paid a pittance. If you're a consumer and you buy stuff from Ikea, you're partly implicated in all this, because this sustains your standard of living. Or look at where your iPod is made the next time you use it. Students use iPods all the time, and they should think about the fact that the person who assembled the iPod would have to use a year of pay, if not more, to buy the iPod. Boycotting these things that are made elsewhere is not the answer, because workers in other countries need the income that comes from export-oriented manufacturing. But if people are aware, then they can try to agitate for more equal conditions of labor throughout the world. Being aware is not in itself a form of freedom. The old idea of consciousness-raising was that knowing you are oppressed makes you free. Teaching people to know how it is that you are deeply implicated, that you are not free, that when you think you are free you are in fact deeply implicated in these structures of exploitation, leads you to try to strive for more freedom, to be less and less implicated. Being completely unimplicated is, I think, an impossible goal, but it should keep people going, as opposed to thinking 'oh, I have my consciousness raised, and therefore I'm free, and therefore I can stop: my conscience is satisfied, and I can sleep easy tonight.'

An interminable goal, if not an achievable one.

The divide between activism and intellectual activity is a false divide. Intellectual activity is also a practice. The victories are not as visible, but you're preparing people who can work towards a victory that might be more visible. So for example if you have students who go to law school, they might decide to enter public law instead of joining a private law firm. That's a small victory, because they might work as a human rights lawyer. Each of us can work in our own arena on behalf of human rights.

If that's a contaminated hope, it's a hope nonetheless, and an edifying culmination of this conversation.

Afsaruddin, Asma. "Views of *Jihad* Throughout History." *Religion Compass* 1:1 (2007): 165-169.

———. "Obedience to Political Authority: An Evolutionary Concept." Paper presented at the Center for the Study of Islam and Democracy, Fourth Annual Conference, 16 May 2003.

Bergen, Peter L. *The Osama bin Laden I Know: An Oral History of al Qaeda's Leader*. Free Press, 2006.

Cheah, Pheng. *Inhuman Conditions: On Cosmopolitanism and Human Rights*. Harvard University Press, 2006.

Cooke, Miriam. *Women and the War Story*. Univ. of California Press, 1996.

———. *Women Claim Islam: Creating Islamic Feminism through Literature*. Routledge, 2001.

Habeck, Mary. *Knowing the Enemy: Jihadist Ideology and the War on Terror*. Yale Univ. Press, 2006.

Kearney, Richard. *On Stories*. Routledge, 2002.

Spahr, Juliana. *Everybody's Autonomy: Connective Reading and Collective Identity*. Univ. of Alabama Press, 2001.

———. *This Connection of Everyone with Lungs*. Univ. of California Press, 2005.

Talarico, Ross. *Once Upon a Time: A Personal Guide to Telling and Writing Your Story*. Story Line Press, 2004.

———. *Spreading the Word: Poetry and the Survival of Community in America*. Duke Univ. Press, 1995.

Woodruff, Paul. *Reverence: Renewing a Forgotten Virtue*. Oxford Univ. Press, 2001.

———. *First Democracy: The Challenge of an Ancient Idea*. Oxford Univ. Press, 2005.

Zarif, M. Javad. "How Not to Inflame Iraq." *New York Times*, 8 February 2007.

———. Statement before the U.N. Security Council, 31 July 2006.

———. "A Neighbor's Vision of the New Iraq." *New York Times*, 10 May 2003.

———. "Reflections on Terrorism, Dialogue and Global Ethics." *Seton Hall Journal of Diplomacy and International Relations* (Winter/Spring 2002): 21-25.

CONTRIBUTORS

Asma Afsaruddin is Associate Professor of Arabic and Islamic Studies at the University of Notre Dame.

Peter Bergen is a terrorism analyst for CNN, a Fellow of the New America Foundation, and an Adjunct Professor at Johns Hopkins University.

Philip Brady, Executive Editor of Etruscan Press, is Professor of English at Youngstown State University and the author of *To Prove My Blood: A Tale of Emigrations & the Afterlife.*

Pheng Cheah is Professor, Department of Rhetoric, University of California, Berkeley.

Miriam Cooke is Professor of Arabic Studies at Duke University.

Mary Habeck is Associate Professor, School of Advanced International Studies, Johns Hopkins University.

Richard Kearney is Professor of Philosophy at Boston College and University College Dublin.

Juliana Spahr's latest book is *The Transformation.*

Ross Talarico is Professor of Writing and Literature at Springfield College, the San Diego campus.

Paul Woodruff is Professor of Philosophy and Dean of Undergraduate Studies at the University of Texas at Austin.

M. Javad Zarif is the current Permanent Representative of the Islamic Republic of Iran to the United Nations.

BOOKS FROM ETRUSCAN PRESS

Chromatic by H. L. Hix (National Book Award finalist)
The Confessions of Doc Williams & Other Poems by William Heyen
Art Into Life: The Craft of Literary Biography by Frederick R. Karl
Shadows of Houses by H. L. Hix
The White Horse: A Colombian Journey by Diane Thiel
Wild and Whirling Words: A Poetic Conversation by H. L. Hix
Shoah Train by William Heyen (National Book Award finalist)
Crow Man by Tom Bailey
As Easy as Lying: Essays on Poetry by H. L. Hix
Cinder by Bruce Bond
Free Concert: New and Selected Poems by Milton Kessler
September 11, 2001: American Writers Respond edited by William Heyen

Etruscan Press
www.etruscanpress.org

Etruscan Press books may be ordered from:

Small Press Distribution
800-869-7553
www.spdbooks.org

Bookmasters
800-345-6665
www.bookmasters.com